John McLemore's

"DADGUM
That's Good!"™ *And Healthy*

Lightened-up Favorites for
Smoking, Frying and Grilling!

Oxmoor House®

AUTHOR: John McLemore
Lifestyle Photos: Tonya McLemore,
    Alicia McGlamory
Story Writer: Alicia McGlamory

OXMOOR HOUSE

Editorial Director: Leah McLaughlin
Creative Director: Felicity Keane
Art Director: Christopher Rhoads
Executive Food Director: Grace Parisi
Senior Editor: Erica Sanders-Foege
Managing Editor: Elizabeth Tyler Austin
Assistant Managing Editor:
    Jeanne de Lathouder

TIME HOME ENTERTAINMENT INC.

President and Publisher: Jim Childs
Vice President and Associate Publisher:
    Margot Schupf
Vice President, Finance: Vandana Patel
Executive Director, Marketing Services:
    Carol Pittard
Publishing Director: Megan Pearlman
Assistant General Counsel: Simone Procas

©2014 by John McLemore and Masterbuilt
www.Masterbuilt.com
Facebook.com/Masterbuilt
Twitter @JohnMcLemore @Masterbuilt

BRAVE INK PRESS

EDITORIAL STAFF
President and Editorial Director:
    Carol Field Dahlstrom
Art Director: Lyne Neymeyer
Food Stylists: Jennifer Peterson,
    Carol Field Dahlstrom
Director, Test Kitchens: Jennifer Peterson
Test Kitchens Professionals:
    Holly Wiederin, Barbara Hoover,
    Elizabeth Dahlstrom, M.S.,
    Crystal Tallman, R.D.
Copy Editor: Liz Burnley
Proofreader: Joyce Trollope
Food Photography: The Wilde Project,
    Jay Wilde; Primary Image, Dean Tanner
Video/Communications:
    Dr. Michael Dahlstrom
BUSINESS STAFF
Business Manager: Judy Bailey
Webmaster: Leigha Bitz
Production Manager: Dave Hollingsworth
Props/Studio Manager: Roger H. Dahlstrom
Marketing/Social Media Manager:
    Marcia Schultz Dahlstrom
www.braveink.com 515-964-1777

ISBN-13: 978-0-8487-4360-4
ISBN-10: 0-8487-4360-1
Library of Congress Control Number:
2014912860

Printed in the United States of America
First Printing 2014

DEDICATED TO DAWSON MCLEMORE

We all have heroes in our lives. Mine was never a comic book character—it was a real man named Dawson McLemore. Dawson is my dad and the hardest working man I've ever known. He taught me if I dreamed about something and worked hard enough for it, I could accomplish it. My favorite Bible verse is Philippians 4:13; Dawson is the epitome of that verse. All of my success began with what my dad started in our backyard when I was a young boy. I dedicate this book to him with thanks for teaching me the most important lesson in life—putting faith and family above all else. I love you, "Ole' Man."

TOP: Me and the Ole' Man
RIGHT: The McLemore Family
LEFT: Dawson, aka "Frosty" with Mr. and Mrs. Claus

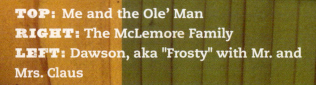

FOREWORD

John and I have always shared a love of comfort food and recipes. His cooking is down-home, soul-warming, and family-friendly. For more years than I can count, John has delighted all of us at QVC with dishes like his Cajun wings, smoked potato salad, his mother's fried chicken, and more. And as much as I've loved the food, I've also enjoyed John's ability to simplify the process behind smoking, grilling, and frying foods—particularly for holidays and big get-togethers, when you're really trying to make an impression and perfect those family favorites.

In this new book, John's taking those same family classics and lightening them up—making them better for all of us without sacrificing flavor. He's shown us that you can make adjustments in your cooking to match your dietary goals without giving up the recipes you've always loved. He's mastered the art of making lighter grilled, smoked, and deep-fried foods, so they're better for our waistlines and better for our overall well-being.

I'm excited to try the very same foods I've always loved, as well as some of his new ones like Smoked Sugary Sausage Wraps, Sweet Corn with Cilantro Chili Butter, Maple BBQ Sliders, and the Grilled Blackberry Cobbler. In fact, I'm headed to my kitchen right now. I've got some cooking to do—and so do you!

–David Venable

TABLE OF CONTENTS

INTRODUCTION

Writing two cookbooks in the last few years has been quite a journey. It's been fun to tour the country and share my recipes. As you'll read in the stories throughout this book, I received a bit of a wake-up call with my health. I was in the beginning stages of planning this book when I received news from my doctor that I needed to make some radical changes in my diet and exercise routine. It didn't take long for me to realize my same old recipes weren't going to cut it anymore. I wanted to continue to enjoy my dadgum good recipes, but I needed to remake them in a new and healthier way. My family is at the heart and root of everything I do and I want to be around for many years to enjoy making memories with them. They're on this healthier path with me and they were excellent test subjects for all of the recipes you'll see here. My hope is you will be able to take this journey also, enjoying dadgum good food all year long without sacrificing your health.

IT'S ALL IN A NAME

If you've followed our journey so far and read my cookbooks, you know the Masterbuilt story. For those who don't know, Masterbuilt is a company my family started in our backyard over 40 years ago, in 1973. We're a cooking products manufacturer and you'd know us from our electric smokers, grills, turkey fryers, and automotive accessories. Growing a backyard business into a worldwide products manufacturer took a lot more than time and hard work—it took a lot of faith. That brings me to a story you may not know—and it's all about the name.

When my dad quit his job with Goodyear Tire and Rubber Company to pursue his American dream of starting a business, he had five children and a wife at home. It wasn't just a leap of faith—it was a bungee jump! He had to decide on a name quickly while applying for a business license at the city office, so he chose M&M Welding—for McLemore and McLemore. A short while later, he was driving down the road and thinking of his family at home and all of the burdens and uncertainty this new business would bring. He pulled over to think and pray. In what he called a frank conversation with the good Lord he said, "If you'll help me with this business, I'll name it after you." And so, in that very moment, the name Masterbuilt came to my father. Our company was "Built by the Master" and we've always said, God is the true CEO of our company; we just run it day by day.

As I've begun a new journey toward physical health, I've realized that it's about more than my body— it's about physical, mental, and spiritual overall health. From Bible studies at Masterbuilt to a quiet moment before a QVC airing or an especially touching moment where my entire company joined together to rally and pray for my brother's health this past year, I'm surrounded by so much love and support. That's something to live long for!

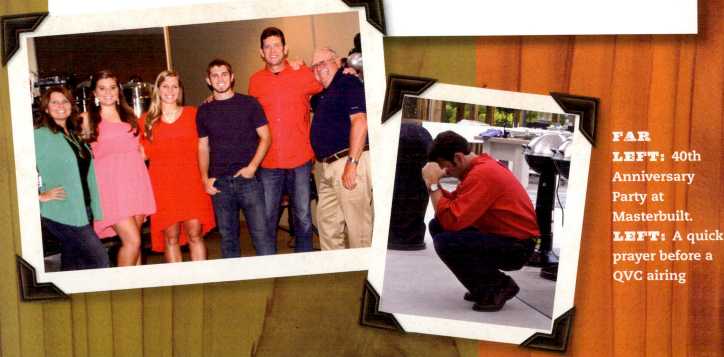

FAR LEFT: 40th Anniversary Party at Masterbuilt. **LEFT:** A quick prayer before a QVC airing

WAKE-UP CALL

If you'd told me 5 years ago that I'd have two best-selling cookbooks and just finished my third, I would have laughed! It's been a crazy and fun journey over the past few years, but my entire life has been full of crazy and fun. I've been surrounded by good Southern food for as long as I can remember, but developing and promoting a couple of cookbooks sure gives you the opportunity to eat more food than you normally would. I packed on a few more pounds than I was comfortable with and when I visited my doctor for a checkup and blood work, I knew she would mention my weight. What I wasn't prepared for was a serious warning about my cholesterol and overall health. She gave me a challenge to radically change my diet over a 3-month period and come back for more blood work. As I'd done many, many times before, I went on a temporary "crash" diet and made sacrifices for a while, thinking I would ace the blood work in 3 months. Well...let's just say this wasn't a high school exam that you studied all night for. You can't crash your way into better

cholesterol numbers and on my return visit my doctor was not pleased with me at all. My numbers were still not good and she explained how some of this is hereditary and I may need to go on medication. For the first time in my life, I knew it was time for a radical lifestyle change, not another temporary adjustment. You see, we lost my mother a few years ago from health complications and I saw her deteriorate over the years. Heart disease and other issues have plagued several members of my immediate family and I didn't want my wife and children to see me go through any of that. I plan to live a long, healthy life—God willing—and this was just the wake-up call I needed.

From that point, I was on a mission. I found a nutritionist and worked on becoming better educated about my overall health and the food choices I was making on a daily basis. My mind has been blown over and over about some of the wrong and downright ignorant food choices I was making. It's been fascinating to learn about all of this, but what's been more exciting is

RIGHT: My reason for getting healthy
FAR RIGHT: Brooke gets engaged!

watching my family go on the journey with me. You see, we've always been a very active, athletic family. You name the sport and we love it and probably play it! We're not a sit back and relax type of family and we're always in motion. Because of all that activity, we allowed ourselves to eat most anything we wanted. Only in recent years have we all seen that our metabolism has caught up with us. For my wife, she's motivated by wanting to live a long, healthy life and she's looking forward to grandchildren. For my daughter Brooke, she's getting married this year and wants to look her very best. My daughter Bailey had a knee injury while skiing and wants to get back in tiptop shape. My son J-Mac, well—he's a 22-year-old guy who can eat anything he wants—but his time will come! Once they knew I needed to make some radical changes, they were all so supportive and asked to follow along with me. We've all been a great source of encouragement for one another, which is exactly what I've needed.

Once I decided to make adjustments, I knew the journey had to be authentic and bleed into every area of my life.

This meant that I had to bring my new choices to work with me. For most of you, that wouldn't be a hard decision. However, when you own a company that manufactures cooking products and you've written two cookbooks full of decadent Southern recipes, well, let's just say it's a bit of a challenge. At Masterbuilt we are constantly cooking, testing recipes, and enjoying dadgum good food at the office. We started to offer healthier alternatives at our company meals. Turkey bacon, oatmeal, yogurt, and egg whites were added to our normal fare during our employee birthday breakfasts. And in my biggest effort to "walk the talk," there's this book. I still want to enjoy dadgum good food, but I needed to remake the recipes in ways that wouldn't negatively affect my health. Remaking all of these favorite recipes from *"DADGUM That's Good!"*™ and *"DADGUM That's Good, Too!"*™ gave me a new way to enjoy the food I love. I'm hoping some part of my journey strikes a familiar chord with you. And don't worry—this isn't yet another diet book. It's a book full of healthier, lighter choices, which is what I'm trying to make every day.

ABOVE: Employee birthday breakfast at Masterbuilt
RIGHT: Masterbuilt Softball Team

MOST COMMON WOODS FOR SMOKING

Whether you are smoking on a small electric smoker on your back porch or a trailer-sized smokehouse, we're sure you can create a dadgum good result with the smoked recipes in this book! When testing a new wood flavor, make sure you begin with a small amount. If you like the flavor, then increase the amount you use when smoking.

▶ **Alder** wood gives off a light flavor that works well with fish and poultry. It makes a perfect pairing with salmon.

▶ **Apple** gives a very sweet, mild flavor to your food. It pairs well with poultry and pork. Apple wood will turn chicken skin dark brown. With this wood, it does take a longer cooking time to infuse the smoke flavor. Be careful not to oversmoke your food, which will result in a bitter taste.

▶ **Cherry** has a mild, sweet flavor and pairs well with most foods. It is great for poultry and fish.

▶ **Hickory** will add a strong smoke flavor; be careful not to overuse. This wood pairs best with pork, beef, and lamb. It is available in most areas.

▶ **Mesquite** is great for smoking and can also be used when grilling. It burns hot and fast, so be prepared to use more wood. Mesquite is a great alternative to hickory and has a milder flavor. It pairs well with most any meat and is especially good for brisket and hamburgers.

▶ **Oak** wood gives a strong smoke flavor without overpowering your food. It pairs well with beef or lamb.

▶ **Pecan** burns cooler than other woods and provides a mild flavor. It pairs well with pork and is a great substitute for hickory.

These woods are used for smoking, but are less common: Almond, Apricot, Ash, Birch, Black Walnut, Citrus (lemon, orange), Crabapple, Grapefruit, Lilac, Maple, Mulberry, Peach, Pear, Plum, Walnut.

Avoid these woods, as they contain sap and will not give off a complementary taste or smell: Cedar, Cypress, Elm, Eucalyptus, Fir, Pine, Redwood, Sassafras, Spruce, Sycamore.

Chips, chunks, logs, or pellets

The cut of wood you choose depends on the type of equipment you use for smoking. For most large barrel-type smokers or charcoal smokers, you'll want to use chunks. Wood chips are most commonly used for propane and electric smokers. Some grills are equipped with an accessory smoker box for adding wood. Pellets are reserved for specialty-type grills or smokers. There is a difference between the type of pellets that are used for a heat source versus pellets used for cooking, so make sure you purchase the correct type. Championship BBQ competitors use very large smokers designed for larger wood logs or chunks.

DIRECT VERSUS INDIRECT GRILLING

▶ **Direct:** Direct grilling is a fast method; the heat is high and the cooking time is shorter. With direct grilling, the food is placed directly above the heat source (charcoal, propane, or electric). This type of grilling method works best for vegetables, hamburgers, or steaks. It's important to stand by your grill when using direct heat and watch the food carefully so it won't burn. Make sure you turn the food as necessary. Close the cover of your grill to get a good sear, but again, don't leave that grill unattended.

▶ **Indirect:** The indirect method of grilling involves placing your food on the grill away from the direct heat source. This means you need to keep your coals or flame off to the side of the food, not directly under it. This is a slower method of grilling, which will require a longer cooking time, but it is much more forgiving. Indirect grilling works great for pork roast, ribs, whole chicken, turkey, and beef brisket.

SMOKING TIMES AND TEMPERATURES

	ITEM	SIZE	TEMP	TIME	INTERNAL TEMP
BEEF	Beef Ribs	Full Rack	225°F	4-5 hours	175°F
	Brisket	6-12 pounds	250°F	1 hour per pound	180°F-190°F
	Roast (Chuck, Sirloin tip)	4-5 pounds	225°F	3-4 hours	145°F Rare 160°F Medium 170°F Well done
GAME	Cornish Game Hens	1.5 pounds each	225°F	4 hours	165°F
	Dove, Pheasant, Quail	12-16 birds	200°F	2-3 hours	180-185°F Well done
	Duck	4-6 pounds	250°F	2.5-4 hours	165°F
PORK	Baby Back Ribs (Unwrapped)	2 slabs	225°F	4-5 hours	165°F
	Baby Back Ribs (Wrapped)	2 slabs	225°F	5-6 hours (Wrapped during last 1.5 to 2 hours)	165°F
	Loin Rib End Roast	4-6 pounds	200°F	4.5-7 hours	170°F Well done (Meat should pull away from bone)
	Loin Roast (Boneless)	3-4 pounds	250°F	2 hours	165°F Well done
	Pork Butt (Sliced)	4-5 pounds	225°F	1- 1.25 hours per pound	165°F
	Pork Butt (Pulled)	4-5 pounds	250°F	1- 1.25 hours per pound unwrapped + .5 hour per pound wrapped	195°F
	Short Ribs	4-5 pounds	200°F	2.5-3.5 hours	165°F
POULTRY	Chicken Breasts (Bone-in)	3 count	225°F	1-1.5 hours per pound	165°F
	Chicken Breasts (Boneless)	3 count	225°F	45 min. per pound	165°F
	Chicken Quarters	4 count	225°F	3-3.5 hours	165°F
	Chicken Thighs	12 count	225°F	2 hours	165°F
	Whole Chicken	3-5 pounds	225°F 250°F	45 min. - 1 hour per pound	165°F
	Whole Turkey	8-12 pounds	225°F	30-35 min. per pound	165°F
SEAFOOD	Fish	2 pounds of fillets	225°F	35-45 minutes	145°F Flakes with a fork
	Salmon	2-3 pounds	200°F	2.5-3.5 hours	145°F Flakes with a fork
	Shrimp	Full Grate	225°F	1-2 hours Based on size of shrimp	145°F Will be pink/shells open
VEGETABLES	Asparagus (fresh)	1.5 pounds	250°F	1.5 hours	Until tender
	Cabbage (fresh)	Whole	250°F	3-4 hours	Until tender
	Green Beans (canned)	2 -14.25 oz. cans	250°F	2 hours	Until tender
	Lima Beans (dried)	1 2-pound package	225°F	8 hours	Until tender
	Sweet Potatoes (fresh)	8 large	275°F	1 hour unwrapped + 1 hour wrapped	Until tender

MEAT

Here are some of the cuts of meat most commonly used:

▶ **Filet Mignon** Cut from the tenderloin, filet is a very tender cut, but lacks the beefy flavor of other cuts. Consider grilling this with a good rub or marinade.

▶ **Flank Steak** A beefy, full-flavored steak cut from the chest and side, this steak is thin and cooks quickly. To retain the juices in the meat, let it rest for a few minutes before carving against the grain.

▶ **Porterhouse and T-Bone** Cut extra thick, these beef cuts give you the taste and texture of the strip and the tenderloin. To prevent them from overcooking, sear the steaks with the strip portion facing the hottest part of the fire and the tenderloin facing the cooler side.

▶ **Rib-Eye Steak** Cut from the rib, they are very tender, beefy, and well-marbled with fat, which makes them great for grilling and smoking. They should be thick and seared over a medium-high heat. Move to a cooler spot on the grill to finish.

▶ **Sirloin, New York Strip, and Prime Rib** Full-flavored premium cuts that have a natural flavor, which you may want to bring out with a little salt, pepper, and olive oil.

▶ **Brisket** The beef brisket consists of two different muscles. The top muscle, known as the "point," is fibrous and difficult to cut. The flat is leaner and more even, which makes it easier to cut. It's likely that you'll find the second cut in your local supermarket, trimmed with a thin layer of fat on the top. If it's untrimmed, trim the fat down to ¼-inch thickness. To test your brisket for tenderness, hold the middle of the brisket in your hand. If the ends give, you've picked the right one. A rigid brisket is a sign that you're in for a tough time.

▶ **Spareribs** Pick ribs that are between 2 and 4 pounds. Smaller ribs are likely to come from a younger animal and will cook faster because they're more tender.

▶ **St. Louis-Style Ribs** These are spare ribs with the sternum bone, cartilage, and rib tips removed to create a rectangular-shaped rack.

▶ **Baby Back Ribs** These flavorsome ribs are great if you're smoking for the first time. Baby backs are a little more expensive, but they're the most tender and cook faster than spareribs.

▶ **Pork Butts and Picnics** Similar cuts with different bones. There is not much difference between them, but they do offer a choice. You can remove the bone or cook them bone-in.

> **TIP** Meat cooked on the bone shrinks less. It also allows you to quickly test for tenderness. When the meat is ready, the bone slides out easily. Buy your pork butt with the fat on and trim it to suit your taste. And remember—fat equals flavor.

FISH

▸ **Mahi-Mahi** Similar in texture to swordfish, but it's a little oilier. Despite this, it dries out quickly on the grill, so you might want to brine it.

▸ **Red Snapper** Quick and easy to grill or fry. If you grill, handle carefully. Make sure the fish and the grill are well oiled.

▸ **Salmon** A favorite for grilling because it doesn't dry out. It's rich in healthy, natural fats, so you can pop it on the grill without oiling. Its flavor also complements stronger marinades.

▸ **Scallops** You'll want to use fresh ocean scallops if you're grilling or frying them. Take a close look at the scallops before you buy them. If they're unnaturally white and are sitting in a milky liquid, they're processed. Natural scallops are a pinkish tan or ivory. They have a firmer texture and a bigger surface area that holds the batter better.

▸ **Trout** Freshwater trout is great on the grill. The skin becomes thin and crispy and the flesh is flavorful without an overpowering fishiness.

▸ **Tuna** does best using a simple marinade of herbs and oil. This prevents it from drying out and getting tough. If you like your tuna rare, buy 1½-inch thick steaks. This will enable you to sear them without overcooking them.

SEAFOOD

▸ **Mussels** Versatile, quick, and cheap. They steam beautifully and within minutes you can rustle up a satisfying gourmet dish.

▸ **Shrimp** taste great any way you cook them. Though some prefer boiled shrimp, there's a lot to be said for steaming them. It retains the delicate flavor better.

> **TIP** Fish smokes fast, so it requires a little more attention. The best types of fish to test in your smoker are salmon and trout fillets. Boneless fish fillets are the easiest to smoke. Fish with a higher fat content, such as trout, salmon, tuna, and mackerel, retain their moisture better during smoking. Most fish should be brined and air-dried before smoking.

▸ USDA* SAFE MINIMUM INTERNAL TEMPERATURES	
Beef, Pork, Veal, and Lamb (Ground)	160°F
Beef, Pork, Veal, and Lamb Steaks, Roasts, and Chops	145°F**
Egg Dishes	160°F
Fish	145°F
Turkey, Chicken, and Duck Whole, Pieces, and Ground	165°F

* United States Department of Agriculture
**plus 3-minute stand time

13

"DADGUM THAT'S GOOD!"™ DRY RUB

Makes about ¾ cup

You'll Need

- 4 tablespoons salt
- 2 tablespoons granulated sugar
- 2 tablespoons paprika
- 2 tablespoons garlic powder
- 2 tablespoons ground celery seeds
- 1 tablespoon freshly ground black pepper
- 1 teaspoon cayenne pepper

Instructions

1. In an airtight container or bowl, combine salt, sugar, paprika, garlic powder, celery seeds, black pepper, and cayenne pepper. Use as a rub on chicken, pork, or beef, or just sprinkle on meat when grilling. Also, use as a seasoning for vegetables when grilling, smoking, or steaming.

"DADGUM THAT'S GOOD!"™ BBQ SAUCE

Makes 2 cups

You'll Need

- 2 tablespoons extra virgin olive oil
- 2 tablespoons minced garlic
- 1 cup ketchup
- 1 cup honey
- ½ cup balsamic vinegar
- ¼ cup soy sauce
- ¼ cup Starbucks® double shot espresso or strong home brewed coffee

Instructions

1. In a medium saucepan over medium heat, combine olive oil and garlic and cook, stirring frequently, until golden, about 20 minutes. Remove from heat and let garlic cool in the oil.

2. Whisk in ketchup, honey, vinegar, soy sauce, and espresso. Return to heat and simmer for 15 minutes to blend flavors. Remove from heat. Serve sauce heated.

"DADGUM THAT'S GOOD!™" BRINE

Makes enough to brine 1 whole chicken or turkey

You'll Need

- 2 cups water
- 2 cups kosher salt
- 2 cups packed brown sugar
- ¼ cup cracked black peppercorns
- 3 tablespoons chopped garlic cloves
- 2 tablespoons chopped fresh basil leaves
- 2 tablespoons chopped fresh rosemary
- 2 tablespoons onion powder
- 1 tablespoon ground ginger
- ½ cup soy sauce
- ½ cup Worcestershire sauce
- 2 gallons ice water

Instructions

1. In a large stockpot, heat 2 cups water with salt, brown sugar, peppercorns, garlic, basil, rosemary, onion powder, ginger, soy sauce, and Worcestershire sauce. Bring to a boil, stirring well. Let cool.
2. When cooled, add 2 gallons ice water, stirring well. Place turkey, chicken, or other meat in a container and pour brining mixture over. Cover and brine in the refrigerator for at least 8 or up to 12 hours. When you remove your meat, rinse it well, inside and out, if necessary, to avoid being too salty after cooking. This is a very important step. After thoroughly rinsing all salt off, pat dry, and cook according to your recipe.

"DADGUM THAT'S GOOD!™" SEASONING

Makes ½ cup

You'll Need

- 2½ tablespoons dark brown sugar
- 1½ teaspoons light brown sugar
- 1 tablespoon paprika
- 1 teaspoon lemon pepper
- ¾ teaspoon onion salt
- ½ teaspoon garlic powder
- ½ teaspoon celery salt
- ½ teaspoon ground ginger
- ½ teaspoon dried basil
- ½ teaspoon crushed sage
- ½ teaspoon cracked black peppercorns
- ¼ teaspoon ground marjoram

Instructions

1. In a medium bowl, combine dark and light brown sugars, paprika, lemon pepper, onion salt, garlic powder, celery salt, ginger, basil, sage, peppercorns, and marjoram. Use as a seasoning on meat or vegetables when grilling, smoking, or steaming.

1
STARTERS

Starters are a great way to kick off an even greater meal, but don't limit yourself to only eating them before a meal. Make an entire menu of starters to add more variety and flavor to your gatherings. Enjoying small portions of many dishes is a fun and healthy alternative to indulging on a huge meal.

RIGHT: My brother Don and me on a fishing trip

GRILLED SALSA

Serves 6

I'm a condiment-lover…the more sauce, the better. I've found that salsa is a perfect "substitute condiment." Salsa adds a ton of flavor to burgers, grilled chicken, and fish, but doesn't add the fat, calories, and sodium of most other condiments or sauces. Don't over-process this salsa—leave it nice and chunky.

Instructions

1. Preheat lightly greased grill to 350°F (medium setting). Slice tomatoes in half and remove membranes and seeds. Grill tomatoes, red onion, garlic, and jalapeño, with grill lid closed, for 5 minutes or until softened and grill marks appear. Remove from grill and let cool.

2. Peel tomatoes and garlic. Remove seeds from jalapeño. In a food processor, combine tomatoes, red onion, garlic, jalapeño, cilantro, lime juice, and salt. Pulse 3 times or until salsa is blended but still chunky. Serve immediately or cover and refrigerate until ready to serve. Serve with tortilla chips.

Grill

You'll Need

- 6 fresh Campari or Roma (plum) tomatoes (about 1 lb.)
- ½ small red onion
- 2 garlic cloves
- 1 fresh jalapeño
- 3 tablespoons chopped fresh cilantro
- 3 tablespoons fresh lime juice
- ¼ teaspoon kosher salt

GOOD FOR YOU

It's important to remove the membrane and seeds from the tomatoes for this salsa. If you don't, it will be too runny. This chunky salsa is full of flavor, fat-free, and packed with vitamin C.

**22 calories
0g fat**

(0g sat fat), 0mg chol, 86mg sodium, 4g carb, 1g fiber, 0g sugar, 1g protein

Grill

You'll Need

- ½ lb. sea scallops (about 10 to 12)
- ¼ teaspoon lemon zest
- 1 teaspoon fresh lemon juice
- ¼ teaspoon sea salt
- ¼ teaspoon freshly ground black pepper
- 10 to 12 slices turkey bacon

GRILLED SCALLOPS IN BACON

Serves 10

As I've been on a mission to lower my cholesterol and still enjoy meals, it was refreshing to discover that scallops are indeed low in cholesterol and fat. Since scallops are one of my favorite foods, I was also pleased to learn that they are rich in omega-3 fatty acids and have other health benefits. Although turkey bacon isn't on my everyday diet, it is still a healthier alternative to pork bacon.

Instructions

1. In a bowl, combine scallops, lemon zest, lemon juice, and ¼ teaspoon each of salt and pepper. Let stand for 15 minutes.

2. Preheat lightly greased grill to 350°F (medium setting). Wrap 1 bacon slice around each scallop, double wrapping the bacon and securing tightly with a toothpick.

3. Grill scallops for 4 to 5 minutes or until scallops are cooked through and bacon is crisp. Serve immediately.

MAKE IT LIGHTER

Grilling the scallops reduces the fat content and brings out their true flavors.

74 calories
3g fat

(1g sat fat), 33mg chol, 334mg sodium, 1g carb, 0g fiber, 0g sugar, 8g protein

Before
173 calories
10g fat

(2g sat fat), 30mg chol, 466mg sodium, 9g carb, 0g fiber, 0g sugar, 11g protein

SMOKED SALMON DIP

Serves 8   *Suggested wood chips for smoking: Apple or Mesquite*

Salmon is one of the easiest fish to smoke, but you have to be very diligent to watch the internal temperature and time so you don't overcook it. Dried-out salmon is a no-go! With this recipe, use our motto of "cook to temp, not time." Don't get stuck on an amount of cooking time—it's done when it reaches 145°F (internal temperature) and flakes with a fork.

Instructions

1. Load the wood tray with one small handful of wood chips and preheat the smoker to 225°F.

2. Lay salmon steaks flat and season them with lemon juice, olive oil, parsley flakes, and Butterball Cajun Seasoning.

3. Place salmon on the middle rack and smoke for 1 to 2 hours, or until internal temperature reaches 145°F. Remove salmon from smoker and let cool.

4. In a large bowl, combine mustard, green onions, pecans, dressing, grapes, and mayonnaise. Crumble salmon steaks into mixture and stir until well mixed. Chill and serve with bagel chips.

Smoker

You'll Need

- 4 to 6 salmon steaks (about 4 lbs.)
- ½ lemon, juiced
- 1 tablespoon extra-virgin olive oil
- 1 tablespoon parsley flakes
- ½ teaspoon Butterball® Cajun Seasoning
- 3 tablespoons Creole mustard
- 2 bunches green onions, sliced
- 1 cup chopped pecans
- ½ cup Greek dressing
- 1 small bunch seedless red grapes, halved
- 2 tablespoons light mayonnaise

MAKE IT LIGHTER

Salmon is a highly nutritious food, loaded with omega-3 fatty acids and high quality protein. It's also heart-healthy and may reduce inflammation.

**669 calories
41g fat**

(7g sat fat), 201mg chol, 439mg sodium, 9g carb, 1g fiber, 1g sugar, 63g protein

**Before
1436 calories
96g fat**

(13g sat fat), 403mg chol, 1866mg sodium, 18g carb, 2g fiber, 3g sugar, 125g protein

ANDREW'S SMOKED GARLIC PEPPER BUFFALO WINGS

Serves 12   *Suggested wood chips for smoking: Apple*

I first met Andrew at QVC when he was there with Rachael Ray. He is a fantastic food stylist and member of Rachael's culinary team. Andrew's a big fan of our Masterbuilt products and I'm glad he's using them to make great recipes like this one. Here are a few thoughts from Andrew: "While I am a properly trained chef and love a fancy meal every now and then, nothing is better to me than great tasting buffalo wings—and I love them in all different forms. For this recipe, I used an awesome rub from one of my favorite spice shops in Chicago called The Spice House. It is their "Back of the Yards Garlic Pepper" rub. You can season with straight salt and pepper, or find a garlic pepper rub from your local spice shop or supermarket. As for the buffalo sauce recipe… use it to make any dish buffalo-style."

Instructions

1. Preheat smoker to 250–275°F. Place chicken wings in a large mixing bowl and drizzle with olive oil. Sprinkle with the garlic pepper rub and toss to combine. Place directly on the smoker rack and cook for about 1 hour to 1 hour 20 minutes, or until fully cooked.

2. While the wings are smoking, place a small sauce pot over low heat and add hot sauce and vinegar. When it starts to steam, whisk in butter, a little chunk at a time until fully incorporated. Season with celery salt and turn off heat. When you're ready to use the sauce, turn heat up to medium for about one minute to bring up to temperature and then turn off.

3. Place cooked wings in a mixing bowl, cover with hot sauce, and toss to combine. Serve with ranch or blue cheese dressing.

Smoker

You'll Need

- 4-5 lbs. chicken wings, about 36 individual pieces
- 1 tablespoon olive oil
- 1 tablespoon garlic pepper rub
- ½ cup hot sauce, such as Frank's Red Hot
- 1 teaspoon white vinegar
- ½ cup (1 stick) butter, cut into chunks
- ¼ teaspoon celery salt
- ½ cup ranch or blue cheese dressing

LEFT: Hanging out with Andrew Kaplan

ALL-TIME FAVORITE

Enjoy these buffalo wings just as they are—they are amazing! If you want a few less calories, choose a low calorie dressing for dipping.

450 calories 37g fat

(2g sat fat), 137mg chol, 744mg sodium, 0g carb, 0g fiber, 0g sugar, 27g protein

Trout fishing isn't an option in our town, but a few hours away are the North Georgia Mountains and parks with streams of trout. We've taken our family there to camp and the kids loved trout fishing. We would ride 4-wheelers to the streams and on one particular trip one of the kids hooked more than a fish, he hooked his friend in the leg! Even when we have little mishaps (or "mis-hooks") we love making new memories with our family.

TOP: Thumbs up for Brooke's catch
ABOVE: I always make Brooke kiss her fish!
RIGHT: 4-wheelin' to the stream with the family

SMOKED TROUT BRUSCHETTA

Serves 8　　*Suggested wood chips for smoking: Hickory or Mesquite*

This appetizer works equally well with trout or mackerel. When selecting your bread for bruschetta, steer clear of lightweight French and Italian loaves with thin crusts and big holes. Look for thick-crusted, dense, whole grain baguettes.

Instructions

1. In a large bowl mix water, low-sodium soy sauce, teriyaki sauce, lemon pepper, garlic salt, and dill weed. Add fillets, cover, and refrigerate for 8 hours or overnight.

2. Load wood tray with one handful of wood chips and preheat the smoker to 225°F. Smoke trout for 55 minutes, until meat is flaky, or until internal temperature reaches 145°F.

3. Cut baguette into 8 diagonal ½-inch thick slices. Place the bread slices about 4 inches from the heat and grill (or broil in oven) for 2 minutes on each side. While still hot, rub bread with garlic and drizzle with oil.

4. In a large bowl, mix tomatoes, parsley, capers, pepper, and salt. Flake the trout with a fork and gently add to tomato mixture. Peel and pit the avocado, then mash. Add lemon juice and mix well. Spread a thin layer of avocado on each slice of bread. Spoon the smoked trout and tomato mixture onto each piece, about ¼ cup per slice. Serve immediately.

Smoker

You'll Need

- 3 cups water
- ¼ cup low-sodium soy sauce
- ¾ cup low-sodium teriyaki sauce
- 2 teaspoons lemon pepper
- ½ teaspoon garlic salt
- 1 teaspoon dill weed
- 4 large trout fillet pieces, or 1 (1 lb.) whole trout
- 1 loaf whole grain baguette
- 3 large garlic cloves, halved
- 3 tablespoons extra-virgin olive oil
- 1¼ lbs. ripe tomatoes, seeded and chopped
- 2 tablespoons fresh parsley, chopped
- 1 tablespoon capers, drained
- ½ teaspoon black pepper
- ½ teaspoon salt
- 1 large avocado
- 1 tablespoon lemon juice

MAKE IT LIGHTER

283 calories
16g fat
(2g sat fat), 40mg chol, 463mg sodium, 16g carb, 4g fiber, 2g sugar, 21g protein

Before
324 calories
16g fat
(2g sat fat), 40mg chol, 710mg sodium, 24g carb, 3g fiber, 3g sugar, 21g protein

Alicia is my Media/PR Manager at Masterbuilt and a great family friend. When I heard she made a mean guacamole, I made sure we included it in our last book. The mark of a good employee is that they go above and beyond the call of duty. Alicia knows I don't care for red onions, so when she's making a batch at the office, she leaves the onions out of mine (or chops them up really fine). Now that's a good employee!

TOP: Alicia's family keeping fit and having fun at an "Electric Run" 5K

ABOVE: Alicia is my hero and I'm wearing the t-shirt to prove it!

RIGHT: Alicia and Tonya all dressed up on the Masterbuilt cruise!

ALICIA'S GUACAMOLE

Serves 4

Everyone loves guacamole and this one is the best! This recipe pairs well with our Flat Iron Steak Tacos (page 114).

Instructions

1. Cut each avocado lengthwise and remove pits. Spoon out avocado flesh and place in a bowl. Pour half of the lime juice over avocado and chop with a spoon so mixture remains chunky.

2. Slice Roma tomatoes lengthwise. Remove and discard seeds and membranes. Chop tomatoes. Add chopped tomatoes, red onion, and fresh cilantro to avocado and stir gently to mix. Pour remaining lime juice over the mixture. Add garlic powder and kosher salt. Serve with favorite chips.

You'll Need

- 2 ripe avocados
- Juice of 2 limes, divided
- 2 Roma (plum) tomatoes
- 2 tablespoons chopped red onion
- 2 tablespoons chopped fresh cilantro
- ⅛ teaspoon garlic powder
- ⅛ teaspoon kosher salt

GOOD FOR YOU

This tasty guacamole is full of healthy unsaturated fats, vitamin E, and lots of flavor!

196 calories
18g fat
(0g sat fat), 0mg chol, 72mg sodium, 7g carb, 3g fiber, 0g sugar, 2g protein

SMOKY SWEET 'N' SPICY WINGS

Serves 12   *Suggested wood chips for smoking: Apple or Pecan*

Try to say that recipe name five times fast! This is yet another popular dish for us. I've cooked these on many regional news shows as we've toured the country. Most news anchors begin the segment by telling me they won't eat on-air. Once the segment begins, without fail, they all cannot resist eating a wing (or two, or three)! I'm so partial to these wings that I chose to smoke them in a local Smoke Off event we sponsored in Columbus, Georgia. I competed against Megan Plummer (wife of Mac from Team Masterbuilt) and a local chef, Jamie Keating.

Instructions

1. In a small bowl, mix together black pepper, onion powder, chili powder, seasoned salt, and garlic powder. Place the chicken wings in a large resealable bag. Pour the dry rub into the bag and shake to coat the wings well. Let stand for 20 minutes at room temperature, or up to 24 hours in the refrigerator.

2. Load the wood tray with one small handful of wood chips and preheat the smoker to 225°F. Place the wings on the top rack of the smoker, and cook for 25 to 30 minutes. Turn wings and cook for another 25 to 30 minutes, or until done.

3. While the wings are cooking, mix the honey, BBQ sauce, and apple juice together in a small saucepan. Cook over medium heat until warmed through. Remove the wings from the smoker and place in a disposable aluminum foil pan. Pour the warm sauce over the wings and toss to coat evenly. Return pan to smoker on middle rack and cook wings for another 25 minutes. Remove from the smoker and serve immediately.

Smoker

You'll Need

- 2½ tablespoons black pepper
- 1 tablespoon onion powder
- 1 tablespoon chili powder
- ½ teaspoon seasoned salt
- 1 tablespoon garlic powder
- 5 lbs. chicken wings, about 36 pieces, rinsed and dried
- ½ cup honey
- ½ cup hot BBQ sauce
- ½ cup apple juice

MAKE IT LIGHTER

257 calories
13g fat

(3g sat fat), 73mg chol, 251mg sodium, 18g carb, 1g fiber, 16g sugar, 17g protein

Before
912 calories
40g fat

(10g sat fat), 220mg chol, 1699mg sodium, 88g carb, 2g fiber, 77g sugar, 50g protein

LEFT: My "cheerleaders" during the Smoke Off

RIGHT: River City Smoke Off with Megan Plummer and Jamie Keating

SIGNATURE RECIPE

Since the press tour for my second cookbook, this dish has been served up by our team more often than any other recipe in the book. Team Masterbuilt travels all over the country, using our products to serve folks at retail Grand Openings and charity events. We make this dish in advance at Masterbuilt and freeze it. It transports well and when we arrive at our destination, we simply thaw and smoke. Don't you just love a dish you can make ahead?

TOP: Team Masterbuilt at Grand Openings event
LEFT: Brooke serves up some Smoky Pimento Cheese Dip.
ABOVE: Alicia preps for another cooking segment.

SMOKY PIMENTO CHEESE DIP

Serves 16   *Suggested wood chips for smoking: Pecan*

Keep a batch or two of this cheesy treat in your freezer for a ready-made appetizer when you have impromptu guests. My wife Tonya doesn't even wait to smoke the dish sometimes—she makes a pimento cheese sandwich right after she mixes the ingredients!

Instructions

1. Preheat smoker to 225°F. In a medium bowl, combine Cheddar cheese, Colby-Jack cheese, Greek-yogurt cream cheese, and cheese spread, mixing well. Add mayonnaise, green onions, pepper, and pimento. Mix until creamy. Place in an 8-inch square baking dish.

2. Place on middle rack of smoker and smoke for 20 minutes. Remove and serve immediately with corn chips, soft French bread cubes, or bagel chips.

Smoker

You'll Need

- 8 ounces sharp reduced-fat Cheddar cheese, grated
- 1 cup grated Colby-Jack cheese
- 8 ounces Greek-yogurt cream cheese, softened
- ¼ cup Cheddar Bacon cheese spread, or your favorite variety
- ¾ cup low-fat mayonnaise
- ¼ cup thinly sliced green onions, green parts only
- ¼ teaspoon coarsely ground black pepper
- 1 4-ounce jar pimento, drained and diced

MAKE IT LIGHTER

Using reduced-fat cheese and yogurt-style cream cheese cuts the calories and fat in this favorite appetizer.

123 calories
8g fat

(5g sat fat), 23mg chol, 314mg sodium, 5g carb, 0g fiber, 4g sugar, 7g protein

Before
320 calories
29g fat

(15g sat fat), 69mg chol, 420mg sodium, 2g carb, 0g fiber, 0g sugar, 12g protein

2

VEGGIES & SIDES

One of the keys to a healthy lifestyle is eating a balanced diet. These alternatives to some all-time favorite sides give you lighter options to complement your main dishes. Cooking veggies and sides in new ways—like grilling and smoking—gives them more flavor.

TOP: Team Masterbuilt with Brandi and Karli Harvey at the Steve Harvey Mentoring Camp in Texas

GRILLED ROSEMARY ZUCCHINI

Serves 4

This grilled zucchini is a flavorful and healthy side dish. Another great option is to use this recipe as a veggie pizza topping on your favorite whole grain crust.

Instructions

1. Preheat lightly greased grill to 350°F (medium setting).

2. In a large shallow dish, combine zucchini, squash, and onion. Sprinkle with salt and pepper. Drizzle with olive oil and lemon juice. Grill vegetables, with grill lid closed, turning occasionally, for 6 to 8 minutes or until tender. Remove from grill and sprinkle with rosemary and feta cheese. Serve warm or at room temperature.

Grill

You'll Need

- 2 medium zucchini (about ¾ lb.), unpeeled and cut into ¼-inch slices

- 1 medium yellow squash, unpeeled and cut into ½-inch slices

- 1 small yellow onion, cut into ½-inch thick rounds

- ½ teaspoon kosher salt

- ¼ teaspoon freshly ground black pepper

- 2 tablespoons olive oil

- 2 tablespoons fresh lemon juice

- 2 tablespoons finely chopped fresh rosemary

- ¼ cup crumbled feta cheese or goat cheese

GOOD FOR YOU

Use a low-fat version of feta cheese if you want to reduce calories even further.

114 calories
9g fat

(2g sat fat), 8mg chol, 409mg sodium, 7g carb, 2g fiber, 4g sugar, 3g protein

2 VEGGIES & SIDES

ABOVE: Hanging with Bob and Sheri after the challenge

RIGHT: Announcing the winner with Todd from *The Bob and Sheri Show*

EGGPLANT FRIES

Serves 10

On our cookbook publicity tours we do quite a bit of radio promotion. One of our favorite shows to do was *The Bob and Sheri Show*. We had some fun with them one day and filmed a "Masterbuilt Chef" competition. I was the judge of three competitors from their station and they each cooked a recipe from my second cookbook. Sheri's submission was Eggplant Fries. I have a special place in my heart for this dish because Momma made them when we were little. Of course, Sheri got my vote and was the winner!

Instructions

1. Place eggplant in a large bowl. Add 2 cups ice and enough water to cover. Cover and refrigerate until chilled, for at least 1 hour.

2. Fill deep fryer halfway with oil and heat to 350°F.

3. In a large bowl, combine cornmeal, garlic powder, and salt. Drain eggplant and dip in cornmeal mixture to coat. Fry eggplant in batches for 3 minutes or until golden brown. Use a metal slotted spoon to transfer to paper towels to drain. Serve immediately.

Fryer

You'll Need

- 1 lb. eggplant, cut lengthwise into ½-inch strips
- 1 gallon cooking oil
- 2 cups white cornmeal
- 1 tablespoon garlic powder
- ½ teaspoon kosher salt

HEALTHY ALTERNATIVE

GRILLED VEGGIES WITH EGGPLANT TOPPERS

Grill some brightly colored vegetables and serve with just a few eggplant fries on the top. You'll add lots of vitamins to your side dish and still get the tasty crispness of the eggplant fries.

79 calories
4g fat

(0g sat fat), 0mg chol, 106mg sodium, 10g carb, 2g fiber, 1g sugar, 2g protein

Recipe based on: ½ cup each of red and green sliced bell pepper, 1 cup sliced eggplant, 1 zucchini sliced, 1 T. olive oil, ¼ t. kosher salt. Toss vegetables in oil. Sprinkle with salt. Grill until tender. Top with fried eggplant slices. (Serves 6)

ALL-TIME FAVORITE

Look for a coarse grind, non-degerminated cornmeal to maximize your intake of whole grains. Choosing a good eggplant can be difficult. Look for one that is firm and heavy for its size, with smooth and shiny skin and a vivid color. The skin of a ripe eggplant should bounce back after you apply slight pressure; if it remains indented, it is probably overly ripe.

204 calories
9g fat

(1g sat fat), 0mg chol, 120mg sodium, 28g carb, 2g fiber, 2g sugar, 2g protein

You'll Need

- ▸ 1 fresh pineapple, sliced
- ▸ 5 tablespoons low-sodium teriyaki sauce

TERIYAKI GRILLED PINEAPPLE

Serves 4

This recipe stands alone as a dadgum good side item. We also have paired it with our Aloha Chicken Sandwich (page 85). Pineapple stands up very well to the grilling process. I recommend using a grilling pan with holes if you have one but you can put it directly on the grill.

Instructions

1. Place pineapple slices in a shallow dish and cover with teriyaki sauce. Marinate in refrigerator for 1 hour.

2. Preheat grill to medium heat. Remove pineapple slices from marinade and grill over medium heat for 3 to 5 minutes on each side. These are great alone or served as a topping on sandwiches and burgers.

GOOD FOR YOU

Pineapple is naturally delicious and a great source for vitamin C. Grilling this favorite fruit brings out the flavor even more!

**95 calories
0g fat**

(0g sat fat), 0mg chol, 251mg sodium, 24g carb, 2g fiber, 18g sugar, 2g protein

BACON-WRAPPED SMOKED ASPARAGUS

Serves 6   *Suggested wood chips for smoking: Hickory*

When smoking vegetables, it's important to limit the amount of smoke so that you don't get a bitter result. Use a small amount of wood chips. If you have a smoker that has been well-seasoned, you may not even have to use wood chips during the process, since there's so much residual smoke already there. The French dressing gives this dish a unique and tangy flavor.

Instructions

1. Wash asparagus and cut the bottom 2 inches off each stalk. Divide into 6 bundles. Wrap each bundle securely with a slice of turkey bacon. Place bundles in a 12-inch square disposable aluminum foil pan. Pour dressing over bundles and cover with aluminum foil. Refrigerate and marinate for 4 hours.

2. Preheat smoker to 250°F. Remove asparagus from refrigerator and discard ½ cup of marinade. Re-cover with aluminum foil and pierce foil with a fork in center and three other places.

3. Place pan on middle rack of smoker and smoke for 45 minutes. Asparagus should be fork-tender. Add one small handful of wood chips to smoker and smoke asparagus for an additional 45 minutes, if you prefer it to be more tender. Remove from marinade and serve.

Smoker

You'll Need

- 1½ lbs. fresh asparagus
- ½ lb. turkey bacon
- 1 (8-ounce) bottle low-fat French dressing

MAKE IT LIGHTER

Eating washed out, limp asparagus is enough to turn even the most avid veggie eater away from this delicate vegetable. Maximize your intake of this vitamin K rich food by choosing asparagus that has tight stalk tips and a firm body. Replacing pork bacon with turkey bacon reduces the fat and calories.

**136 calories
9g fat**

(2g sat fat), 34mg chol, 529mg sodium, 8g carb, 2g fiber, 4g sugar, 8g protein

**Before
264 calories
19g fat**

(6g sat fat), 42mg chol, 987mg sodium, 7g carb, 2g fiber, 4g sugar, 17g protein

BOBBY DEEN'S GRILLED CORN WITH PIMENTO CHEESE

Serves 8

I met Bobby at QVC and we instantly connected as Georgia boys. We share so much in common with our love of both food and family. He's a great example of taking Southern favorite dishes and remaking them in a healthier way. Thanks to Bobby for sharing this recipe, which combines two of my favorite foods—corn and pimento cheese.

Instructions

1. Grease a grill grate with cooking spray, and preheat the grill to medium-high heat.

2. Using a handheld mixer, beat the cream cheese until fluffy. Beat in the Cheddar cheese, mayonnaise, pimentos, Worcestershire, onion powder, and pepper until combined.

3. Place the ears of corn on the grill and cook, covered, turning them occasionally, until tender, 10 to 15 minutes.

4. Spread 2 tablespoons of the pimento cheese over each ear of corn, and serve with the lime wedges.

RIGHT: Tonya with Bobby at QVC

Grill

You'll Need

- 2 tablespoons low-fat cream cheese (Neufchatel), at room temperature
- 1 cup shredded low-fat Cheddar cheese
- 3 tablespoons light mayonnaise
- 1½ teaspoons jarred chopped pimentos, mashed with fork
- ¼ teaspoon Worcestershire sauce
- Pinch of onion powder
- Freshly ground black pepper to taste
- 8 ears corn, shucked
- Lime wedges, for serving

2 VEGGIES & SIDES

GOOD FOR YOU

Corn on the grill is a summer treat! By choosing low-fat toppings, you can enjoy this favorite vegetable with fewer calories.

124 calories
4g fat

(1g sat fat), 6mg chol, 160mg sodium, 18g carb, 2g fiber, 3g sugar, 7g protein

You'll Need

- 1 lb. carrots, peeled and cut into 1-inch pieces
- 1 head cabbage, chopped
- 1 tablespoon extra-virgin olive oil
- 1 teaspoon kosher salt
- 1 teaspoon coarsely ground black pepper
- 1 tablespoon dried basil leaves

CABBAGE 'N' CARROTS

Serves 6

Another option for cooking carrots is to smoke them. Smoke carrots and cabbage at 275°F for 45 minutes to an hour, until tender. You'll say it is dadgum good either way!

Instructions

1. Preheat grill to medium heat. Place cabbage and carrots in a large bowl. Sprinkle with extra-virgin olive oil and toss to coat evenly.

2. Spread cabbage and carrots onto a grill pan or a double-layer of aluminum foil. Sprinkle with salt, pepper, and dried basil leaves.

3. Grill over medium heat for 10 to 15 minutes, stirring occasionally, until tender.

GOOD FOR YOU

Carrots are an excellent source of vitamin A. Carrots also contain fiber, vitamin K, potassium, folate, manganese, phosphorous, magnesium, vitamin E, and zinc. Rich in vitamin K, 1 cup of cabbage provides 85 percent of the body's daily requirement.

85 calories
5g fat
(1g sat fat), 0mg chol, 377mg sodium, 9g carb, 4g fiber, 0g sugar, 2g protein

GRILLED PORTABELLA MUSHROOMS

Serves 3

When my doctor put me on notice about my cholesterol and overall health, one of the things I was asked to cut out was red meat. As a guy who loves burgers and steaks, this wasn't the best news. A grilled portabella mushroom burger gives me a healthier alternative without sacrificing a filling and satisfying meal. Grilled onions make a great companion to this "meaty" vegetable.

Instructions

1. Whisk together vinegar, water, Stevia, garlic, cayenne pepper, and olive oil to make marinade. Place marinade and mushroom caps in a resealable plastic bag. Marinate in refrigerator for 1 hour, turning once.

2. Preheat grill to 325°F (medium setting). Grill mushrooms over indirect heat, 5 minutes on each side (begin with cap side down first). Baste several times with marinade while grilling.

Grill

You'll Need

- ⅓ cup balsamic vinegar
- ½ cup water
- 1 tablespoon Stevia
- 1 clove garlic, minced
- ¼ teaspoon cayenne pepper
- 2 tablespoons olive oil
- 3 large portabella mushroom caps

GOOD FOR YOU

Portabella mushrooms have a moderately high amount of fiber; a 100-gram serving contains just over 2 grams. Fiber is a key nutrient for controlling cholesterol and blood-sugar levels. It also has a filling effect on the body, which is beneficial for weight maintenance.

129 calories
9g fat

(1g sat fat), 0mg chol, 12mg sodium, 10g carb, 1g fiber, 6g sugar, 2g protein

You'll Need:

- 4 to 6 cups fresh Brussels sprouts, sliced thin
- ¼ cup olive oil
- ½ teaspoon kosher salt
- 1 teaspoon onion powder
- 1 teaspoon garlic powder

GRILLED BRUSSELS SPROUTS

Serves 6

Brussels sprouts sure do get a bad rap—from kids turning up their nose to hiding them in their napkins! I wonder if most of that bad reputation comes from being prepared the wrong way. They can have a slightly bitter taste if not seasoned and cooked properly. Of all the possible cooking methods for Brussels sprouts, grilling has to be my favorite. The grilling process chars the sprouts and gives them a sweet and savory flavor. Make sure you have a grill pan or use heavy-duty foil for this recipe so you don't lose the sprouts through the grill grates. My kids call these mini-cabbages. Whatever you call them, they are dadgum good!

Instructions

1. Preheat the grill to 350°F (medium to medium-high setting).

2. Slice Brussels sprouts as thin as possible, and place in a bowl. Toss gently with olive oil. Sprinkle with kosher salt, onion powder, and garlic powder.

3. Use a grill pan or double-layer of heavy-duty foil. Place sprouts on the pan/foil on the grill. Grill for 15 to 20 minutes, turning frequently. Some pieces will be crisp and charred, which enhances the flavor.

GOOD FOR YOU

As far as vegetables go, Brussels sprouts are relatively high in protein (although not a complete protein) at 3 grams per serving, and low in calories at just 38 calories per cup. Brussels sprouts' major health advantages come from their fiber and vitamin content, being rich in both vitamins C and K.

117 calories
9g fat
(1g sat fat), 0mg chol, 216mg sodium, 8g carb, 3g fiber, 2g sugar, 3g protein

KARLI AND BRANDI'S GRILLED VEGGIES

Serves 4

It's been fun to appear on Steve Harvey's television show several times and I've enjoyed getting to know him better. Outside of his work in entertainment, he has a real passion for mentoring young men with his Steve Harvey Mentoring Camp. We were honored to serve at the camp and feed the young men and volunteers. Steve's daughters Brandi and Karli do such great work with the Steve and Marjorie Harvey Foundation. They've been a real joy to work with and we even found out they love to grill dadgum good food together. Be sure to check out www.smharveyfoundation.org for more information on the good work they do to mentor and foster excellence in children.

Instructions

1. Preheat the grill to 350°F (medium to medium-high setting). Place all vegetables in a large bowl, sprinkle with seasonings, and toss. Drizzle olive oil and balsamic vinegar over vegetables and toss vegetables again. Make sure all veggies are covered with oil, vinegar, and spices.

2. Grill 5 to 10 minutes or until tender. Remove from grill. Cut into bite-size pieces.

RIGHT: Brandi and Karli Harvey with our family

Grill

You'll Need

- 1 box (8-ounces) whole mushrooms
- 1 medium zucchini, halved lengthwise
- 1 medium summer squash, halved lengthwise
- 1 red bell pepper, seeded and halved
- 1 medium onion, sliced
- ½ teaspoon salt
- ½ teaspoon black pepper
- ½ teaspoon paprika
- ¼ teaspoon garlic powder
- 1 tablespoon fresh rosemary
- 1 tablespoon fresh thyme
- 2 tablespoons olive oil
- 2 tablespoons balsamic vinegar

2 VEGGIES & SIDES

GOOD FOR YOU
115 calories
7g fat
(1g sat fat), 0mg chol, 304mg sodium, 11g carb, 3g fiber, 7g sugar, 4g protein

You'll Need

- 2 large tomatoes
- ½ teaspoon olive oil
- ¼ teaspoon steak seasoning
- ⅓ cup freshly grated Parmesan cheese

GRILLED TOMATOES

Serves 4

We mention the benefits of indirect grilling throughout this book. You can reference our grilling tips on page 10 for more detailed info on direct versus indirect grilling. This is definitely a recipe that requires the indirect method of grilling. Even though you are placing the tomatoes on foil, make sure you position them away from the heat source. This allows them to cook without scorching the skin.

Instructions

1. Cut tomatoes in half, then score the inside membrane with a knife several times. Drizzle tomatoes with olive oil. Sprinkle with steak seasoning and Parmesan.

2. Preheat lightly greased grill to 350°F (medium setting).

3. Place tomatoes on a sheet of heavy-duty aluminum foil. Place foil with tomatoes on grill and grill over indirect heat, with grill lid closed, for 25 to 45 minutes. Check halfway through grilling, so the Parmesan cheese does not burn.

MAKE IT LIGHTER

Lycopene is a powerful antioxidant that protects against disease. When tomatoes are cooked, especially in a fat such as olive oil, the lycopene is more completely absorbed.

63 calories
4g fat
(2g sat fat), 7mg chol, 435mg sodium, 3g carb, 1g fiber, 0g sugar, 5g protein

Before
83 calories
5g fat
(2g sat fat), 10mg chol, 510mg sodium, 3g carb, 1g fiber, 0g sugar, 7g protein

TONYA'S GREEN BEANS

Serves 4

My wife Tonya is famous in our family for her Green Bean Casserole and Fried Green Beans. She's been such a good sport to go along with my healthier choices lately and in an effort of solidarity she changed up the way she cooks green beans. This recipe is a much lighter alternative to her usual green bean fare. Since we spend so much time outside, we like to grill this recipe, as well. Just make sure you use a grill-safe pan. These green beans are so good we don't even miss the casserole. Well....maybe just a little!

Instructions

1. Wash and snap the ends off the green beans.

2. Heat the olive oil in pan over medium heat.

3. Add the green beans and cover. Cook for 15 minutes, stirring often.

4. Add salt and pepper and serve.

Stove Top

You'll Need

- ▶ 1 lb. fresh whole green beans
- ▶ 2 tablespoons olive oil
- ▶ ¼ teaspoon kosher salt
- ▶ Black pepper to taste

ABOVE: Still doing our best to stay a strong and healthy duo!

GOOD FOR YOU

Green beans are a rich source of vitamins, minerals, and other plant-derived micronutrients. They are also a great source of dietary fiber.

96 calories
7g fat

(1g sat fat), 0mg chol, 128mg sodium, 6g carb, 3g fiber, 3g sugar, 2g protein

You'll Need

▸ 4 ears corn, husked

Cilantro Chili Butter:

▸ ¼ cup butter, softened

▸ 1 tablespoon seeded and finely chopped fresh jalapeño

▸ ¼ cup fresh cilantro, chopped

▸ ¼ teaspoon ground cayenne pepper

▸ 1 teaspoon grated lime zest

▸ 1 teaspoon lime juice

▸ ½ teaspoon onion powder

▸ 1 clove garlic, minced

MAKE IT LIGHTER

Corn is one of the most commonly eaten vegetables in America but can be overlooked for its nutritional content. Corn is a good source of insoluble fiber and tastes great with or without added butter or fat.

201 calories
13g fat

(7g sat fat), 30mg chol, 16mg sodium, 18g carb, 3g fiber, 3g sugar, 3g protein

Before
515 calories
47g fat

(29g sat fat), 121mg chol, 21mg sodium, 19g carb, 3g fiber, 3g sugar, 4g protein

SWEET CORN WITH CILANTRO CHILI BUTTER

Serves 4

Given a choice, I would eat unlimited amounts of corn. I could seriously eat corn, prepared any way, for every meal—including breakfast! I learned from my nutritionist that I need to limit corn, as it's a starchy veggie, but that it's still a good source of fiber. If I'm going to limit one of my favorite foods that means I want it cooked in the most delicious way possible. Steaming corn allows it to keep the nutrients and color and the aroma is so sweet! The cilantro chili butter is the perfect complement.

Instructions

1. Fill Butterball® or Masterbuilt fryer to the MAX fill line with water. Set to 375°F and bring to a boil. This will take approximately 15 to 20 minutes. Although cooking time on this recipe is short, water may need to be added if steamer is used for more than 60 minutes. Using the drain clip, hook the basket on the inner pot.

2. Husk corn and rinse. Coat the steamer basket with nonstick cooking spray or line with a layer of corn husks. (Note: Do not lower basket into water when steaming.) Cover and steam the corn for 30 minutes.

Cilantro Chili Butter:

Mix butter, jalapeño, cilantro, cayenne, lime zest, lime juice, onion powder, and garlic in a medium bowl. Place butter mixture on rectangular piece of wax paper, roll into a cylinder, and freeze. To serve, slice the butter into 1-inch medallions. Place a medallion of butter on each piece of steamed corn.

STEAMED VEGETABLES

Serves 8

My nutritionist is doing her best to educate me on healthier eating options and she's got her job cut out for her! One of the facts I've learned is that I can "load up" on vegetables if they are the non-starchy kind. In this version of the recipe, we added broccoli, which makes this dish fit the bill! Simple additions and replacements like this make a ton of difference in your overall health.

Instructions

1. Fill Butterball® or Masterbuilt fryer to the MAX fill line with water. Set to 375°F and bring to a boil. This will take approximately 15 to 20 minutes. Although cooking time on this recipe is short, water may need to be added if steamer is used for more than 60 minutes.

2. In the steamer basket, layer sliced red potatoes first, then carrots, then squash, then broccoli, and finally the onion. Lightly sprinkle each layer with sea salt and pepper. (Note: Do not lower basket into water when steaming.)

3. Cover and steam at 375°F, until the potatoes are done and the carrots are tender but still crisp, approximately 6 to 8 minutes. Remove vegetables from steamer and place into a large serving bowl; toss with the extra-virgin olive oil to coat, and serve warm.

Fryer/Steamer

You'll Need

- 2 lbs. red potatoes, unpeeled, cut into 1/2-inch slices
- 6 carrots, sliced 1/4-inch thick
- 2 lbs. squash, cubed
- 1 cup broccoli florets
- 2 large onions, sliced 1/4-inch thick
- Sea salt and black pepper to taste
- 2 tablespoons extra-virgin olive oil

2 VEGGIES & SIDES

GOOD FOR YOU

Steaming cruciferous veggies such as broccoli and cauliflower is a good way to reduce some of the bitterness commonly associated with these types of vegetables. Cruciferous vegetables are some of the most potent cancer-fighting vegetables in existence.

180 calories
4g fat

(1g sat fat), 0mg chol, 58mg sodium, 31g carb, 5g fiber, 8g sugar, 5g protein

You'll Need

- 2 lbs. sweet potatoes, cut into 1-inch chunks
- 3 ripe pears, peeled, cored, and diced
- 2 tablespoons butter
- ½ teaspoon ground cinnamon
- ¼ teaspoon ground nutmeg
- 1 teaspoon ground cardamom
- 2 teaspoons finely chopped ginger root
- ½ teaspoon salt
- ¼ teaspoon black pepper

SPICED SWEET POTATOES

Serves 8

In my quest to eat healthier, my vegetable consumption has increased greatly. It can be difficult to find new ways to enjoy veggies without getting bored with the same old flavors. This combination of sweet potatoes and pears is amazing!

Instructions

1. Fill Butterball® or Masterbuilt fryer to the MAX fill line with water. Set to 375°F and bring to a boil. This will take approximately 15 to 20 minutes. Although cooking time on this recipe is short, water may need to be added if steamer is used for more than 60 minutes.

2. Coat steamer basket with nonstick cooking spray and add the sweet potatoes. Using the drain clip, hook the basket onto the inner pot. (Note: Do not lower basket into water when steaming.) Cover and steam for 25 minutes, or until soft enough to mash.

3. In a medium skillet, sauté pears, butter, cinnamon, and nutmeg until pears caramelize, about 2 minutes.

4. Transfer steamed sweet potatoes to a large bowl and coarsely mash, adding cardamom, ginger, salt, and pepper. Stir in the sautéed pears. Place the mixture into a shallow casserole dish, and bake in a preheated 350°F oven until heated through, about 15 to 20 minutes.

ITALIAN-STYLE PEPPERS

Serves 6

Sometimes when grilling peppers, it is good to cook them near the heat source. For stuffed peppers, however, you'll want to use the indirect grilling method. Place the peppers away from the direct heat source so that they slowly grill to perfection.

Instructions

1. Peel eggplants and cut into 1-inch cubes. Layer in a colander, sprinkling each layer with salt. Place the colander over a sink and let the eggplant drain for approximately 1 hour.

2. Spray a 13x9-inch baking pan with cooking spray. With a small knife, cut off the very top of the peppers, removing seeds and membranes. Stand peppers on end in the pan.

3. Preheat grill to 350°F (medium setting). Rinse the drained eggplant and pat dry with paper towels. In a large skillet, heat chicken broth over medium heat. Cook eggplant until tender, about 10 minutes. Stir in the tomatoes, olives, anchovies, capers, garlic, parsley, and pepper. Simmer and cook for 5 minutes. Stir in ½ cup panko and remove from heat. Stuff the peppers evenly with the eggplant mixture. Sprinkle peppers with remaining panko; drizzle with olive oil. Pour 1 cup water into the pan around the peppers.

4. Grill, covered, for 1 hour until peppers are lightly browned and slightly crispy.

Grill

You'll Need

- ▸ 2 medium eggplants
- ▸ 1 teaspoon salt
- ▸ 6 large red, green, and/or yellow bell peppers
- ▸ ½ cup low-sodium chicken broth
- ▸ 3 medium tomatoes, peeled, seeded, and chopped
- ▸ 1 cup black olives, pitted
- ▸ 3 anchovy filets, finely chopped
- ▸ 3 tablespoons capers, rinsed and drained
- ▸ 1 large clove garlic, finely chopped
- ▸ 3 tablespoons fresh parsley, chopped
- ▸ ½ teaspoon black pepper
- ▸ 1 cup panko bread crumbs
- ▸ 2 tablespoon olive oil
- ▸ 1 cup water

MAKE IT LIGHTER

241 calories
8g fat

(1g sat fat), 2mg chol, 458mg sodium, 38g carb, 11g fiber, 12g sugar, 7g protein

Before
421 calories
28g fat

(4g sat fat), 3mg chol, 534mg sodium, 38g carb, 11g fiber, 12g sugar, 7g protein

SMOKED MAC & CHEESE

Serves 6 *Suggested wood chips for smoking: Hickory*

When we told Team Masterbuilt about writing a healthier cookbook, we challenged them to present us with their own light versions of our recipes. Katie was the first to respond with her version of our Smoked Mac & Cheese. Nancy Kitts' original recipe from *"DADGUM That's Good, Too!"* is packed with flavor and calories, but it is an all-time favorite for us all. Katie's version gives you the flavor, but is more waistline-friendly. So now we have two recipes to share! We've promised our friend David Venable at QVC that we'd always have some mac & cheese in our books!

Instructions

1. Preheat smoker to 275°F. Cook macaroni according to package directions, adding olive oil to the water before boiling to avoid sticking. Drain and rinse with warm water. Add Velveeta and Cheddar cheeses, sour cream, mayonnaise, onion powder, and Cajun seasoning; stir together well.

2. Place mixture in a greased 11x7-inch disposable aluminum foil pan and top with crushed cheese crackers. Place in smoker and smoke for 1 hour. Remove from smoker and enjoy.

Note: It's not necessary to use wood chips if your smoker is well-seasoned and you would like a lighter smoke flavor.

Smoker

You'll Need

- ► 1 package (8-ounces) elbow macaroni
- ► 1 teaspoon extra-virgin olive oil
- ► 4 ounces Velveeta Cheese, grated
- ► 4 cups grated Cheddar cheese
- ► 1 cup sour cream
- ► 1 cup Hellmann's mayonnaise
- ► 1½ teaspoons onion powder
- ► ½ teaspoon Cajun seasoning
- ► 1½ cups crushed cheese crackers

ABOVE: Katie and I at a trade show

HEALTHY ALTERNATIVE

KATIE'S LOW-FAT MAC & CHEESE
Katie substituted low-fat cheeses and whole grain pasta for this great-tasting, lower-fat version of smoked mac & cheese.

374 calories
10g fat
(5g sat fat), 28mg chol, 877mg sodium, 44g carb, 4g fiber, 4g sugar, 27g protein

Recipe based on: 1 package (8-ounces) whole wheat elbow macaroni, 1 t. extra-virgin olive oil, 4 ounces grated Velveeta Light cheese, 2 cups grated low-fat sharp Cheddar cheese, 1 carton (15-ounces) light Ricotta cheese, 1 cup plain non-fat Greek yogurt, ¼ cup low-fat mayonnaise, 1 t. onion powder, ½ t. Cajun seasoning, 1 cup crushed, unsalted whole wheat crackers. Mix and smoke as for original recipe. (Serves 6)

ALL-TIME FAVORITE

909 calories
68g fat
(29g sat fat), 92mg chol, 1237mg sodium, 43g carb, 2g fiber, 4g sugar, 29g protein

3
SOUPS & SALADS

Soups and salads are usually really good for you, but they can pack tons of extra sodium or calories. The healthy options in this chapter have lots of flavor and variety without sneaking in extra fat, sodium, and calories.

TOP: Thumbs up for another taste test in MeMaw's kitchen
ABOVE: Backstage with Sunny Anderson

SMOKED POTATO SALAD

Serves 6   *Suggested wood chips for smoking: Hickory*

In the South, you're likely to find potato salad at any gathering of friends and family. In fact, it's on most Southern restaurant menus. Cooked the traditional way, potato salad is anything but a healthy option. This recipe is a lighter way to enjoy a good ol' Southern favorite.

Instructions

1. Load the wood tray with one small handful of wood chips and preheat the smoker to 225°F.

2. Peel potatoes and place them in a large saucepan with water to cover and boil for 20 minutes, until just tender. Drain potatoes and dry them on a plate layered with paper towels.

3. Place potatoes directly on the smoker racks and close smoker door. Reduce heat to 200°F and add more wood chips every 45 minutes. Keep potatoes in smoker for 2 hours. Remove potatoes from smoker and dice them for the salad.

4. In a large bowl, mix onion, pickles, boiled eggs, mayonnaise, vinegar, mustard, salt, and pepper to taste. Add diced potatoes to the mixture. Cover and chill salad in the refrigerator for several hours before serving.

Smoker

You'll Need

- 1½ lbs. russet potatoes, peeled
- ½ cup finely diced red onion
- ½ cup chopped crisp, tart pickles
- 3 hard-cooked eggs, coarsely chopped
- ⅓ cup light mayonnaise
- 2 tablespoons cider vinegar
- 1 tablespoon Dijon mustard
- Salt and black pepper to taste

3 SOUPS & SALADS

GOOD FOR YOU

Potatoes are a good source of potassium and vitamin C, and eggs are high in protein. So enjoy this salad year around!

175 calories
7g fat

(2g sat fat), 112mg chol, 288mg sodium, 23g carb, 2g fiber, 3g sugar, 5g protein

GRILLED GREEK CHICKEN SALAD

Serves 4

Because my family and I have very busy lives, we have to eat out much more than I care for. Making healthy choices in restaurants can be daunting, but with the help of our nutritionist we have become more educated on those choices. My wife Tonya frequently orders Greek salads and loves that particular combination of flavors. This recipe helps satisfy her Greek salad cravings at home, too!

Instructions

1. In a medium bowl, combine dill, olive oil, red onion, garlic, lemon zest, lemon juice, and fennel. Place this mixture and the chicken in a resealable plastic bag and marinate for 1 to 4 hours in refrigerator.

2. Preheat grill to 350°F (medium setting). Remove chicken from marinade. Place chicken breasts on grill and cook 8 minutes on each side.

3. Place remaining marinade in a small saucepan and bring to a boil. Baste chicken with marinade. Turn and grill another 4 minutes each side, or until the internal temperature reaches 165°F. Remove from grill, and salt and pepper to taste. Wrap in aluminum foil until cool.

Salad:

1. In a large salad bowl, combine lettuce, tomato, cucumber, red onion, feta cheese, and black olives.

2. In a food processor, combine vinegar, oregano, salt, and pepper, and mix on high. Add olive oil in a slow stream while mixing. When dressing is well-mixed, lightly drizzle over the salad and toss.

3. Divide salad between plates. Top each serving with a breast of chicken.

Grill

You'll Need

- ½ cup dill, chopped
- ¼ cup extra-virgin olive oil
- 1 small red onion, sliced
- 3 garlic cloves, crushed
- Zest of 1 lemon
- Juice of 1 lemon
- 1 teaspoon crushed fennel
- 4 skinless, boneless chicken breast halves

Salad:

- 2 hearts romaine lettuce
- 1 large tomato, cubed
- 1 cucumber, cubed
- 1 small red onion, sliced
- 1 cup feta cheese, cubed
- 1 cup black olives
- ¼ cup red wine vinegar
- 1½ teaspoons dried oregano, crushed
- ½ teaspoon salt
- ¼ teaspoon black pepper
- ½ cup extra-virgin olive oil

3 SOUPS & SALADS

GOOD FOR YOU

517 calories
41g fat
(5g sat fat), 85mg chol, 835mg sodium, 10g carb, 1g fiber, 1g sugar, 27g protein

SMOKED SALMON CHOWDER

Serves 6   *Suggested wood chips for smoking: Alder*

When you think of smoked salmon, "comfort food" is probably not a category that comes to mind. We've made salmon so comfortable here it's curled up with a blanket on the couch watching a classic movie!

Instructions

1. Load the wood tray with one small handful of wood chips and preheat the smoker to 225°F.

2. Reduce smoker temp to 200°F and place salmon directly on rack. Smoke for 40 minutes at 200°F, or until internal temperature reaches 145°F.

3. In a large stockpot, combine the butter, olive oil, onion, garlic, and celery. Cook over medium-high heat for 8 to 10 minutes, or until the onions are transparent. Sprinkle flour over the mixture and stir well to make a dry roux. Gradually add the water and stir until liquid thickens slightly. Add chicken bouillon cubes and stir in the potatoes, dill, tarragon, thyme, and paprika. Reduce heat to medium, cover, and simmer for 18 to 20 minutes or until potatoes are tender.

4. Remove any skin from the smoked salmon, flake and add to the stockpot. Stir in the lemon juice, hot sauce, salt, pepper, and milk. Simmer over low heat, uncovered, for 10 minutes, stirring occasionally. Do not let the chowder boil after adding the milk. Serve hot.

ABOVE: Ready for some comfort food!

Smoker

You'll Need

- 8 ounces fresh salmon, cut into ½-inch pieces
- 1 tablespoon butter
- 1 tablespoon extra-virgin olive oil
- 1 cup chopped onion
- 2 garlic cloves, finely chopped
- ½ cup chopped celery
- ½ cup all-purpose flour
- 5 cups water
- 2 low-sodium chicken bouillon cubes
- 1 lb. red potatoes, cubed
- 1 teaspoon dried dill weed
- 1 teaspoon dried tarragon
- 1 teaspoon dried thyme
- ½ teaspoon paprika
- 1 tablespoon fresh lemon juice
- ¼ teaspoon hot sauce
- ½ teaspoon salt
- 1 teaspoon black pepper
- 1 cup 2% milk

MAKE IT LIGHTER

235 calories
9g fat
(3g sat fat), 42mg chol, 573mg sodium, 23g carb, 2g fiber, 2g sugar, 15g protein

Before
415 calories
21g fat
(9g sat fat), 85mg chol, 1280mg sodium, 33g carb, 3g fiber, 2g sugar, 21g protein

3 SOUPS & SALADS

DUCK SALAD WITH CITRUS DRESSING

Serves 6

Duck is a fatty bird, so part of the challenge with any duck recipe is to cut the fat off or find ways of letting the fat drain during the cooking process. If you're cooking the breast or the whole bird, you'll need to score the skin. When scoring the skin, lightly cut the surface and into the fat. Don't cut down into the meat, or you'll end up with a dry bird.

Instructions

1. Load the wood tray with one small handful of wood chips and preheat the smoker to 225°F.

2. Prepare the duck by pouring boiling water over the skin to render some of the fat. Place duck in the smoker and cook at 225°F for 1 hour per pound. Smoke until duck breast reaches an internal temperature of 165°F. Remove from smoker, remove skin, and slice into thin strips. Set aside.

Dressing:

1. In a medium bowl, mix orange juice, lemon juice, vinegar, sugar, sesame oil, chives, salt, and pepper. Pour into a dressing bottle or suitable container and shake.

2. Place lettuce on serving plates and top with sliced duck. Drizzle dressing over the salad and serve. Garnish with tomatoes and orange slices, if desired.

ABOVE: Our family at a Peking Duck restaurant in China

Smoker

You'll Need

▸ 1 duck breast, skin on

Dressing:

▸ ⅓ cup orange juice

▸ 3 tablespoons fresh lemon juice

▸ 2 tablespoons rice wine vinegar

▸ 1 tablespoon sugar

▸ 2 tablespoons sesame oil

▸ 1 tablespoon chopped fresh chives

▸ ½ teaspoon kosher salt

▸ ¼ teaspoon black pepper

▸ 1 bag (5-ounces) fresh mixed lettuce

3 SOUPS & SALADS

GOOD FOR YOU

Topping fresh greens with slices of smoked duck is a great way to combine rich flavor with good nutrition.

**126 calories
7g fat**

(1g sat fat), 43mg chol, 242mg sodium, 4g carb, 0g fiber, 3g sugar, 11g protein

You'll Need

- 1 whole chicken
- 1 tablespoon olive oil
- 1 medium onion, chopped
- 2 jalapeños, chopped
- 2 red chile peppers, chopped
- 2 garlic cloves, chopped
- 3 cups low-sodium chicken broth
- 2 cans low-sodium navy beans, rinsed and drained
- 2 cans (each 14.5 ounces) low-sodium diced tomatoes
- 3 teaspoons chili powder
- 1 teaspoon ground cumin
- 1 teaspoon dried oregano
- ½ teaspoon cayenne pepper
- Shredded reduced-fat Monterey Jack cheese

SMOKY CHICKEN CHILI

Serves 6   *Suggested wood chips for smoking: Apple*

Our test kitchen at Masterbuilt is called "MeMaw's Kitchen" (named after my momma). On any given day, the employees of Masterbuilt are working hard in the kitchen to test recipes. This was one of the more popular dishes we tested for this cookbook. Folks kept coming back for seconds and there were a lot of sad faces when we ran out. In fact, we ended up making a whole new batch the next day. We didn't need to test the recipe anymore; we just needed to satisfy the masses!

Instructions

1. Preheat smoker to 225°F. Smoke chicken for 4 to 5 hours until internal temp is 165°F. "Pull" or shred the chicken and set aside.

2. In a large stockpot, add the oil. Over medium-heat, sauté the onion, jalapeño peppers, red chile peppers, and garlic for about 10 minutes.

3. Add the chicken broth, shredded chicken, navy beans, diced tomatoes, chili powder, cumin, oregano, and cayenne pepper to the stockpot. Bring to a boil. Reduce heat to low and simmer for 1 hour. Top each serving with 2 tablespoons of shredded Monterey Jack cheese and enjoy!

GOOD FOR YOU

463 calories
18g fat
(4g sat fat), 150mg chol, 867mg sodium, 19g carb, 6g fiber, 4g sugar, 55g protein

TURKEY SALAD WITH HAZELNUTS

Serves 10   *Suggested wood chips for smoking: Hickory*

When you own a company that makes turkey fryers, you eat quite a bit of turkey—cooked every which way! Honestly, our turkey is always so dadgum good, we don't typically have leftovers. BUT, if you do, this is the perfect recipe for using up those turkey extras.

Instructions

1. In a large container, combine the salt, brown sugar, syrup, apple juice, and water. Mix the brine well. Place turkey in brine and refrigerate for 12 to 24 hours.

2. Load the wood tray with one small handful of wood chips and preheat the smoker to 250°F. Remove the turkey breast from brine and pat dry with paper towels. Reduce smoker temperature to 225°F. Place the turkey breast in the smoker and cook for 25 to 30 minutes per pound, or until inside meat temperature reaches 165°F. Remove turkey breast from smoker and let rest for 15 minutes before carving.

3. In a medium bowl, mix sliced or chopped turkey, green onions, celery, mayonnaise, 2 tablespoons of thyme, and lemon juice.

4. To make the vinaigrette, whisk oil, vinegar, and the remaining thyme in a large mixing bowl. Season with salt and pepper to taste. Add greens to the vinaigrette mixture and toss. Divide among plates. Top greens with cherries and nuts and serve.

Smoker

You'll Need

- 1 cup kosher salt
- 1 cup packed brown sugar
- ½ cup maple syrup
- 2 quarts apple juice
- 2 quarts water
- 1 (5 lb.) turkey breast
- 1 cup chopped green onions
- ½ cup chopped celery
- ¾ cup low-fat mayonnaise
- 3 tablespoons fresh thyme, chopped
- 2 tablespoons lemon juice
- 6 tablespoons extra-virgin olive oil
- 3 tablespoons white wine vinegar
- 1 package (8-ounces) mixed baby greens
- 1 cup dried cherries, chopped
- ½ cup toasted hazelnuts, coarsely chopped

3 SOUPS & SALADS

MAKE IT LIGHTER

**533 calories
29g fat**

(9g sat fat), 136mg chol, 754mg sodium, 18g carb, 2g fiber, 11g sugar, 50g protein

**Before
1952 calories
96g fat**

(31g sat fat), 453mg chol, 2514mg sodium, 103g carb, 10g fiber, 60g sugar, 169g protein

"I love making a vinaigrette in a big ol' Mason or Ball jar and keeping it on hand in the fridge for roasted vegetables or fruit salads during cookouts. Sometimes I roast vegetables for fajitas or pizzas and work the leftover odds and ends into a salad. This is my favorite combination with one of my trusty vinaigrettes that I keep on hand all grilling season. I toss it with vegetables here, but it's equally delicious over fresh strawberries, tossed with chunks of roasted pineapples, and peaches. Enjoy!"   – *Sunny*

RIGHT: With Sunny and Rachael after the Buffalo Ranch-giving

SUNNY'S CHARRED VEGETABLE SALAD

Serves 6

I met Sunny at the *Rachael Ray Show* and we became instant friends! We've since appeared on QVC and Rachael's show again. Thanks to my friend, Sunny, for sharing this great recipe. Read some of her tips on the opposite page.

Instructions

Vegetables:

1. Preheat the grill to 400°F. Place the vegetables on a baking sheet; drizzle with the olive oil. Season with a pinch of salt and a few grinds of pepper. Put vegetables on the direct heat of the grill, with the head of cauliflower floret side down. Allow to char, then rotate until they become golden and charred on all sides, about 24 minutes total. (Remove items to a plate as they char; the cauliflower will take the longest.)

2. Remove the bell peppers to a bowl and cover with plastic wrap to steam for at least 5 minutes. Allow the vegetables to cool before handling. Cut the cauliflower down to florets and toss them in a large bowl. Pull the charred skin off the bell peppers, remove the seeds and stems, then finely chop to a ¼-inch dice and add to the bowl. Finely chop the scallions and add to the bowl.

Vinaigrette: In a glass jar with a lid, add mustard, rosemary, sage, garlic, lemon zest and juice, honey, liquid smoke, paprika, and olive oil. Seal jar and shake vigorously until everything is combined. Taste the vinaigrette and season with a pinch of salt.

Salad: To the large bowl of vegetables add the parsley and red onion. Add just enough vinaigrette to coat; there may be some left over. Using your hands, gently toss the vegetables with the vinaigrette. Serve slightly warm or at room temperature.

GOOD FOR YOU

Grilled vegetables add flavor to any salad. Vinaigrette dressings have fewer calories and fat than creamy dressings.

320 calories
27g fat

(4g sat fat), 0mg chol, 120mg sodium, 17g carb, 6g fiber, 9g sugar, 5g protein

Grill

You'll Need

Vegetables:

- 2 heads cauliflower, whole with outer leaves trimmed off
- 1 whole red bell pepper
- 1 whole yellow bell pepper
- 2 scallions
- ¼ cup olive oil
- Kosher salt and black pepper to taste

Vinaigrette:

- 2 teaspoons grained Dijon mustard
- 2 teaspoons dried rosemary, crushed and rubbed by hand
- 2 teaspoons dried whole leaf sage, crushed and rubbed by hand
- 2 garlic cloves, finely minced or grated on a rasp
- Zest of 2 lemons
- ¼ cup fresh lemon juice
- 2 teaspoons honey
- ½ teaspoon liquid smoke, hickory or mesquite
- ½ teaspoon hot Hungarian paprika
- ½ cup olive oil
- Kosher salt to taste

Salad:

- ½ cup fresh whole parsley leaves, not chopped (lightly packed)
- ½ cup red onion sliced paper thin on a mandolin

You'll Need

- 2 flat anchovy filets, drained
- 2 garlic cloves
- ⅓ cup extra-virgin olive oil
- ¼ teaspoon salt
- ¼ teaspoon black pepper
- 1 large pasteurized egg or ¼ cup liquid pasteurized egg, such as Egg Beaters
- 2 tablespoons fresh lemon juice
- 12 slices multigrain baguette, sliced into 12½-inch slices
- 4 romaine hearts, halved
- ½ cup finely grated Parmigiano-Reggiano cheese

GRILLED CAESAR SALAD

Serves 4

Caesar salad is one of those sneaky salads. You can assume you're eating healthy, but prepared the wrong way it can have a lot of calories, carbs, and the like. Limiting dressing amounts and croutons is a good ways to cut the negative and still enjoy a classic salad recipe.

Instructions

1. Preheat grill to 350°F (medium setting). To make the dressing, combine anchovies, garlic, oil, salt, and pepper in a food processor, then process on high until smooth. Add egg and lemon juice and process until combined.

2. Brush both sides of baguette slices with dressing. Place bread slices on aluminum foil and grill, turning once, 3 to 4 minutes each side, or until toasted. Cut romaine hearts in half lengthwise, and grill with cut sides down for 2 minutes. Do not turn. Remove from grill. Chop romaine crosswise into 2-inch strips, and transfer to a medium mixing bowl. Cut the grilled baguette slices into ½-inch cubes and add to romaine, along with the Parmigiano-Reggiano cheese. Toss and serve immediately with remaining salad dressing.

MAKE IT LIGHTER

Replacing white bread with a multigrain baguette increases the fiber content, and the oil in the dressing contains several grams of healthy unsaturated fats.

462 calories
26g fat
(5g sat fat), 66mg chol, 655mg sodium, 37g carb, 9g fiber, 6g sugar, 20g protein

Before
675 calories
37g fat
(8g sat fat), 77mg chol, 1065mg sodium, 61g carb, 6g fiber, 6g sugar, 25g protein

PINEAPPLE RICE SALAD

Serves 6

A bowl of this rice salad would be perfect for a light lunch on it's own. It also serves as the perfect companion to our Jamaican Jerk Chicken on page 143.

Instructions

1. In a food processor or blender, combine sunflower oil, sesame oil, pineapple juice, garlic, red pepper flakes, soy sauce, fresh pineapple, and ginger. Purée until smooth. Transfer to a small saucepan and gently warm just before serving. Do not simmer or boil.

2. Place arugula on a medium platter. Set aside for later.

3. In a large skillet over medium heat, combine the green onions, shallots, and cashews. Add half of the dressing and sauté until heated throughout. Stir in rice.

4. Spoon the rice mixture over the arugula and drizzle with remaining dressing. Finish with a sprinkle of green onion.

Stove Top

You'll Need

- 2 tablespoons sunflower oil
- 2 tablespoons toasted sesame oil
- ¼ cup canned pineapple juice
- 1 garlic clove
- ¼ teaspoon red pepper flakes
- 1 tablespoons reduced sodium soy sauce
- 1 cup fresh pineapple, cut into chunks
- 2 teaspoons freshly grated ginger
- 4 cups packed arugula
- 4 green onions, thinly sliced
- 3 shallots, peeled and thinly sliced
- ½ cup unsalted, roasted cashews, chopped
- 2 cups cooked brown rice, room temperature

MAKE IT LIGHTER

288 calories
16g fat
(2g sat fat), 0mg chol, 145mg sodium, 31g carb, 3g fiber, 5g sugar, 5g protein

Before
429 calories
29g fat
(4g sat fat), 0mg chol, 634mg sodium, 34g carb, 3g fiber, 5g sugar, 8g protein

MEXICAN STEAK SALAD

Serves 6

One of the secrets to perfect flank steak is actually patience. When the steak is done on the grill, allow it to rest for about 10 minutes in foil to achieve perfect, juicy results. I also enjoy this recipe the next day as a cold steak salad. If you have a more expensive cut of steak, you can use it for this recipe, but an inexpensive flank steak is all you need.

Instructions

Steak:

1. In a small bowl, combine all the rub ingredients and mix well. Coat the flank steak liberally on both sides. Refrigerate uncovered for 2 hours.

2. Grill steak on high heat for 8 minutes on each side, until internal temperature reaches 145°F. Remove from grill, wrap in aluminum foil, and let rest for 10 minutes. When the steak cools, slice into fine strips against the grain.

Dressing: Combine lime juice, cilantro, sugar, chili powder, and salt in a blender and blend at high speed. While the blender is running, add the olive oil in a slow stream until the dressing emulsifies.

Salad: Place the chopped lettuce on a large platter; add sliced avocado, carrots, tomato, cheddar cheese, black beans, and olives. Add strips of steak on top and gently mix salad while adding the dressing.

Grill

You'll Need

- 1½ lbs. beef flank steak

Dry Rub:

- 2 garlic cloves, finely chopped
- 1 tablespoon chili powder
- 2 teaspoons ground cumin
- ¼ teaspoon salt
- ½ teaspoon black pepper

Dressing:

- ¼ cup fresh lime juice
- ½ cup fresh cilantro, chopped and stems removed
- 1 teaspoon sugar
- 1 tablespoon chili powder
- ¼ teaspoon salt
- ⅓ cup extra-virgin olive oil

Salad:

- 1 head romaine lettuce, chopped
- 1 firm, ripe avocado
- ¾ cup shredded carrots
- 1 large tomato, chopped and seeded
- ¾ cup extra-sharp cheddar cheese, grated
- 1 can (15-ounce) black beans, drained and rinsed
- ½ cup black olives, drained, pitted, and sliced

3 SOUPS & SALADS

MAKE IT LIGHTER

Using less cheese and adding shredded carrots reduces the fat and sodium in this recipe while adding fiber and vitamin A.

663 calories
35g fat
(8g sat fat), 57mg chol, 805mg sodium, 47g carb, 14g fiber, 4g sugar, 40g protein

Before
1719 calories
123g fat
(28g sat fat), 172mg chol, 2848mg sodium, 59g carb, 22g fiber, 10g sugar, 94g protein

4
SANDWICHES & SLIDERS

Portion size is one way to make healthier choices. Sliders offer a more petite way to enjoy the flavor of larger burgers and sandwiches. Making simple swaps with your bread choices are also an easy way to trim calories and carbs. Open-face sandwiches are a good choice as well. These recipes make moderation tasty and fun!

TOP: Scuba diving in Jamaica on a family trip
RIGHT: Masterbuilt's CFO Glenn and his wife Nancy

CHICKEN AVOCADO BURGERS

Serves 6

These burgers taste fantastic when grilled or smoked. If you choose to smoke them, don't let the appearance fool you. Ground chicken has a light color and you may think they are underdone at first glance. Carefully monitor the internal temperature—they are done when they reach 165°F.

Instructions

1. Preheat grill to 325°F (medium setting).

2. Gently toss the chicken, avocado chunks, panko, garlic, jalapeño, salt, and pepper together. Form mixture into patties, being careful not to mash the avocado chunks.

3. Grill patties for 20 minutes, turning halfway through the cooking time. Internal temp should be 165°F. Serve on whole grain sandwich thins with lettuce and tomato.

Option: Smoke these burgers for approximately 1 hour at 275°F degrees, until internal temp is 165°F.

Grill

You'll Need

- 1 lb. ground chicken
- 1 large ripe avocado, cut into small chunks
- ½ cup panko bread crumbs
- 2 garlic cloves, chopped
- 1 jalapeño, chopped
- Salt and pepper to taste
- Whole grain sandwich thins
- Lettuce leaves
- Sliced tomatoes

GOOD FOR YOU

When most people think of potassium sources, they think of bananas. In fact, one avocado has nearly double the amount of potassium as a banana. Consuming enough potassium daily can help control blood pressure.

336 calories
12g fat

(3g sat fat), 64mg chol, 415mg sodium, 38g carb, 9g fiber, 3g sugar, 21g protein

SMOKED SHRIMP PO' BOYS WITH REMOULADE SAUCE

Serves 8   *Suggested wood chips for smoking: Alder*

The name po' boy on these sandwiches originates from a time in New Orleans when workers on strike were fed these sandwiches and they were referred to as "poor boys." Well, no matter if you're po', rich, or anything in-between, you're gonna love these sandwiches.

Instructions

1. In water tray, add liquid shrimp boil, bay leaves, and water. Preheat smoker to 250°F.

2. Place shrimp in a 13x9-inch baking dish or a disposable aluminum foil pan and drizzle with lemon juice. In a small saucepan over medium heat, melt butter. Add Worcestershire sauce, Cajun seasoning, and garlic pepper, mixing well. Pour over shrimp.

3. Place shrimp on middle rack of smoker, uncovered. Reduce smoker to 225°F and smoke for about 50 minutes. Remove from smoker and place under oven broiler to broil shrimp to lightly brown, about 3 minutes.

Rémoulade Sauce:

1. In a food processor, combine oil, yogurt, mustard, horseradish, lemon juice, parsley, red wine vinegar, paprika, and garlic; purée until smooth.

2. Spread rémoulade sauce over each side of bun. Place shredded lettuce, several slices of tomato, and dill pickle slices on each. Mound shrimp on each sandwich and enjoy!

Smoker

You'll Need:

- 1 teaspoon liquid shrimp boil
- 3 bay leaves
- ½ cup water
- 4 lbs. large shrimp, peeled, deveined, and washed
- Juice of 3 lemons
- 3 tablespoons butter
- 1 tablespoon Worcestershire sauce
- ½ teaspoon Cajun seasoning
- 1 tablespoon garlic pepper
- 6 po' boy wheat buns
- 3 cups shredded iceberg lettuce
- 3 large tomatoes, thinly sliced
- ¼ cup thinly sliced dill pickles

Rémoulade Sauce:

- ¼ cup vegetable oil
- ¼ cup plain Greek yogurt
- 1 tablespoon Creole mustard
- 2 tablespoons horseradish sauce
- 2 tablespoons fresh lemon juice
- 1 tablespoon fresh parsley
- 2 teaspoons red wine vinegar
- 1 teaspoon paprika
- 2½ teaspoons minced fresh garlic

> ## MAKE IT LIGHTER
>
> Using plain Greek yogurt in the rémoulade sauce keeps the fat and calories down and gives the sauce a tangy flavor that complements the shrimp.
>
> **527 calories**
> **16g fat**
> (4g sat fat), 350mg chol, 861mg sodium, 41g carb, 8g fiber, 7g sugar, 55g protein
>
> **Before**
> **930 calories**
> **39g fat**
> (13g sat fat), 420mg chol, 1131mg sodium, 67g carb, 5g fiber, 8g sugar, 75g protein

4 SANDWICHES & SLIDERS

ALOHA CHICKEN SANDWICH

Serves 6

One of the adjustments I've had to make when grocery shopping is with the marinades I buy. Previously, I always migrated toward dark, high-sodium marinades. Now, I take the time to read labels and it's been refreshing to see that there are many healthy alternatives to choose from. The sesame orange marinade for this chicken adds great flavor without sacrificing my healthy goals.

Instructions

1. Place chicken breasts in a shallow dish. Cover with Drew's marinade and marinate in fridge for 1 to 4 hours.

2. Remove chicken from marinade and grill at 325°F (medium setting) for 4 to 5 minutes on each side.

3. Place grilled chicken on whole grain bread and top with Teriyaki Grilled Pineapple slices. Serve.

Grill

You'll Need:

- 1½ lbs. boneless, skinless chicken breasts (6 pieces)
- 1 cup Drew's All-Natural Sesame Orange Salad Dressing or mixture of 1 cup orange juice and 2 tablespoons sesame oil
- Teriyaki Grilled Pineapple slices (see page 42 for recipe)
- 12 slices whole grain bread

GOOD FOR YOU

Check the label when buying chicken and choose breasts or tenders that have not been processed with salt. This will help keep the sodium content lower.

413 calories
15g fat

(3g sat fat), 94mg chol, 431mg sodium, 26g carb, 4g fiber, 5g sugar, 41g protein

4 SANDWICHES & SLIDERS

You'll Need

- 1 lb. ground chicken
- 1 jalapeño, chopped
- 1 red chili pepper, chopped
- 2 garlic cloves, chopped
- 1 teaspoon Cajun seasoning
- 6 small whole grain buns

KICKED UP CAJUN CHICKEN SLIDERS

Serves 6   *Suggested wood chips for smoking: Apple*

You don't have to be from Louisiana to love and enjoy the flavors of Cajun food. In fact, around Masterbuilt, Cajun seasoning is one of our most popular spices. It packs a whole lot of flavor and adds just the right amount of "kick" (just as the name says) to most recipes. If you want to add even more kick, increase the amount of jalapeño.

Instructions

1. Gently toss the chicken, jalapeño, red chili pepper, garlic, and Cajun seasoning together.

2. Form mixture into patties.

3. Smoke burgers for approximately 1 hour at 275°F, until internal temperature reaches 165°F.

4. Serve burgers with hot sauce, on a whole grain bun with mixed greens and red onion or desired toppings.

Option: Grill patties at 325°F (medium setting) for 20 minutes, turning halfway through the cooking time. Internal temperature should be 165°F.

GOOD FOR YOU

When most people think of getting iron into their diets, they automatically think of beef. However, chicken is also a great source of iron and an inexpensive way to add more to your diet.

282 calories
9g fat

(2g sat fat), 64mg chol, 492mg sodium, 33g carb, 7g fiber, 3g sugar, 20g protein

TUNA BURGERS

Serves 8

Grilling these burgers to the proper internal temp is crucial. While some meats can be very forgiving and still flavorful when overcooked a bit, tuna is not one of them. Buying fresh tuna is another key to success with this recipe.

Instructions

1. In a large bowl, combine tuna, capers, eggs, shallots, mustard, thyme, rosemary, salt, and pepper. Shape tuna mixture into 8 patties, each ¾-inch thick, and place on a plate. Cover and refrigerate for 1 hour.

2. Spray grill rack with nonstick spray. Preheat grill to 350°F (medium setting). Place burgers on grill and cook 4 minutes per side, until internal temperature reaches 160°F.

3. Spread roll bottoms with Olive Spread. Top each with burger, tomato, onion, and arugula.

Olive Spread: In a mini food processor, chop the olives, olive oil, shallots, mint, thyme, and lemon juice. Season olive spread with salt and pepper to taste.

You'll Need

- 2 lbs. fresh tuna steaks, finely diced and chilled
- 2 tablespoons capers, drained and chopped
- 2 eggs, beaten
- 2 tablespoons shallots, chopped
- 1 tablespoon Dijon mustard
- 1 teaspoon minced thyme
- 1 teaspoon fresh minced rosemary
- ¼ teaspoon salt
- 1 teaspoon black pepper
- 8 (4-inch) wheat rolls
- 1 large tomato, sliced
- 1 onion, thinly sliced
- 2 cups baby arugula

Olive Spread:

- ¾ cup purple olives, pitted
- 3 tablespoons extra-virgin olive oil
- 2 tablespoons shallots, chopped
- 2 tablespoons fresh mint, chopped
- 2 teaspoons fresh thyme, chopped
- 2 teaspoons fresh lemon juice

4 SANDWICHES & SLIDERS

GOOD FOR YOU

**315 calories
14g fat**

(3g sat fat), 96mg chol, 403mg sodium, 16g carb, 3g fiber, 3g sugar, 31g protein

You'll Need

- ▸ 4 (6-ounce) salmon fillets (skin on)
- ▸ 1 teaspoon vegetable oil
- ▸ 6 sub or hoagie rolls

BBQ Sauce:

- ▸ 1 tablespoon vegetable oil
- ▸ ¼ cup onion, finely minced
- ▸ 1 garlic clove, finely minced
- ▸ ½ cup low-sodium ketchup
- ▸ 1 tablespoon Tabasco chipotle sauce
- ▸ 1 teaspoon Worcestershire sauce
- ▸ ½ teaspoon dry mustard
- ▸ 1 tablespoon cider vinegar

Coleslaw:

- ▸ 2 tablespoons low-fat mayonnaise
- ▸ 1 tablespoon plain Greek yogurt
- ▸ 1 tablespoon cider vinegar
- ▸ 2 cups coleslaw mix
- ▸ 1½ tablespoons cilantro
- ▸ Salt and black pepper to taste

MAKE IT LIGHTER

**415 calories
21g fat**

(4g sat fat), 62mg chol, 380mg sodium, 28g carb, 2g fiber, 7g sugar, 28g protein

**Before
636 calories
38g fat**

(7g sat fat), 97mg chol, 1973mg sodium, 33g carb, 2g fiber, 12g sugar, 40g protein

SALMON SUBS

Serves 6

Grilled salmon is as good for you as it tastes because it's high in omega-3 oils. Lightly oil your grill grates, preheat, and cook the salmon skin side up, allowing the natural fat under the skin to be drawn into the fillet.

Instructions

1. Preheat grill to medium-high heat. Rub salmon fillets with oil; sprinkle with salt and pepper to taste. Grill salmon skin side up for 4 minutes. Turn and brush with BBQ sauce.

2. Continue to grill until skin is crisp and fish is cooked through, for 6 minutes, or until the meat of the fish is opaque in color. Remove and place on a platter; discard salmon skin. Toast buns on grill; place salmon on bun. Brush with BBQ Sauce and top with Coleslaw. Serve with remaining sauce.

BBQ Sauce: In medium skillet, heat vegetable oil on medium heat; add onions and garlic, and sauté until soft. Reduce heat and add ketchup, Tabasco sauce, Worcestershire sauce, mustard, and vinegar. Cook for 2 minutes. Cool the sauce and purée in a blender. Pour into a small bowl and set sauce aside.

Coleslaw: Whisk mayonnaise, yogurt, and vinegar in a medium bowl. Add coleslaw mix and cilantro. Season with salt and pepper, mixing coleslaw well. Refrigerate until the salmon is cooked.

SMOKED CHICKEN SALAD SANDWICHES

Serves 8   *Suggested wood chips for smoking: Apple*

Without a doubt, this recipe has been one of the most popular from my previous books. In fact, we've heard numerous times that it's the best chicken salad folks have ever eaten! It has become our game-day go-to menu item. Why? Because you can make this ahead the day before, assemble your sandwiches while watching the game, and enjoy!

Instructions

1. Preheat smoker to 225°F. Fill water tray with water and add bay leaves. Brush chicken with vinaigrette dressing and place on middle rack of smoker and smoke for 45 minutes per pound or until internal temperature reaches 165°F.

2. Meanwhile, place pecans in a small disposable aluminum foil pan and pour melted butter over top. Stir well to coat pecans. Place pan on top rack of smoker during the last half of smoking time for the chicken. Smoke pecans for 30 minutes. Remove from smoker and drain on a paper towel. Remove chicken. Let cool, then chop.

3. In a large bowl, combine chopped chicken, pecans, celery, and dried cranberries. Add mayonnaise and yogurt. Season with Cajun seasoning and pepper. Fill pita with red lettuce and chicken salad and serve.

Smoker

You'll Need

- ▸ 3 bay leaves
- ▸ 3 large boneless skinless chicken breasts
- ▸ 2 tablespoons vinaigrette dressing
- ▸ ¾ cup pecans, very coarsely chopped
- ▸ 1 tablespoon butter, melted
- ▸ 1 cup finely chopped celery
- ▸ 1 bag (5-ounce) dried cranberries
- ▸ ¾ cup low-fat mayonnaise
- ▸ ¼ cup plain Greek yogurt
- ▸ ¼ teaspoon Cajun seasoning
- ▸ ½ teaspoon freshly ground black pepper
- ▸ 8 half whole grain pita breads
- ▸ Red leaf lettuce

4 SANDWICHES & SLIDERS

MAKE IT LIGHTER

360 calories
14g fat

(2g sat fat), 55mg chol, 489mg sodium, 35g carb, 5g fiber, 13g sugar, 25g protein

Before
737 calories
55g fat

(11g sat fat), 80mg chol, 1355mg sodium, 48g carb, 4g fiber, 15g sugar, 15g protein

The "thumbs-up" symbol has been a signature of our family for as long as I can remember. In most every photo we take, someone (or everyone!) has a thumbs-up. In my last book, this sandwich was a favorite of my wife Tonya's, and she's given this new version her seal of approval, too!

TOP: Tonya gives a thumbs-up when her carriage arrives.
ABOVE: The kids striking a thumbs-up pose
RIGHT: Thumbs-up from J-Mac and famliy after his bike accident

THUMBS-UP FRIED GREEN TOMATO SANDWICHES

Serves 4

Instructions

1. Place oil in bottom of skillet. In a medium bowl, combine cornmeal, flour, panko, and pepper. Place eggs in a shallow dish. Dip tomatoes in egg and then in cornmeal mixture.

2. Fry tomatoes in batches, turning once, for 2 minutes or until lightly browned. Use a metal slotted spoon to transfer to paper towels to drain.

3. Place bread slices on a work surface. Spread 4 slices equally with Spicy Yogurt Spread. Top equally with bacon, mixed greens, and green tomatoes. Top with remaining bread slices.

Spicy Yogurt Spread: In a small bowl, combine yogurt, lemon juice, Dijon, bell pepper, pickle relish, green onions, and hot sauce. Use immediately as a sandwich spread or cover and refrigerate for up to 2 days.

Stove Top

You'll Need

- 4 tablespoons olive oil
- ½ cup self-rising cornmeal
- ¼ cup all-purpose flour
- ¼ cup whole wheat panko bread crumbs
- ¼ teaspoon black pepper
- 2 eggs, lightly beaten
- 2 green tomatoes, thinly sliced
- 8 slices whole grain bread
- 4 slices turkey bacon
- ½ cup mixed greens

Spicy Yogurt Spread:

- ½ cup plain Greek yogurt
- 1 tablespoon fresh lemon juice
- 1 tablespoon Dijon mustard
- 1 tablespoon chopped red bell pepper
- 2 teaspoons pickle relish
- 2 teaspoons chopped green onions
- ½ teaspoon hot sauce

4 SANDWICHES & SLIDERS

MAKE IT LIGHTER

**370 calories
14g fat**

(3g sat fat), 118mg chol, 733mg sodium, 40g carb, 5g fiber, 9g sugar, 20g protein

**Before
1242 calories
63g fat**

(11g sat fat), 130mg chol, 1987mg sodium, 138g carb, 7g fiber, 8g sugar, 32g protein

GRILLED GROUPER SANDWICHES

Serves 4

Every time I eat grouper, I think of the time I was spearfishing in Panama City Beach, Florida. I was about 13 years old and we were scuba diving outside of the jetties. I speared a grouper and he took me on a good five minute ride around the ocean. I didn't want to lose my spear gun or that fish! In the end, I kept my spear gun and the fish was served up for dinner. That fish ride was so much fun, I went right back for more the very next day!

Instructions

1. Place vinaigrette dressing in large shallow dish. Brush fillets with dressing and let stand for at least 10 minutes. Drain fish.

2. Preheat grill to 350°F (medium setting). Grill fish for 6 to 8 minutes or until fish flakes easily when tested with fork. Remove from grill and serve on buns with Greek Yogurt-Lime Topping and desired toppings such as lettuce, pickles, and sliced tomatoes.

Greek Yogurt-Lime Topping:

In a medium bowl, combine Greek yogurt, lime juice, pickles, onion, parsley, and jalapeño. Cover and refrigerate until serving for up to 2 days.

Grill

You'll Need

- 2 lbs. fresh grouper fillets, cut into 4 equal pieces
- ½ cup vinaigrette dressing
- 4 sandwich buns, toasted

Greek Yogurt-Lime Topping:

- ⅓ cup plain Greek yogurt
- 2 tablespoons fresh lime juice
- 1 tablespoon chopped sweet pickles
- 1 tablespoon chopped red or yellow onion
- 1 tablespoon chopped fresh Italian parsley
- 1 teaspoon chopped jalapeño

LEFT: Team Masterbuilt after a fishing trip

BELOW: J-Mac also enjoys spear fishing.

MAKE IT LIGHTER

Ounce for ounce, fish is comparable to beef and pork as a great source of protein.

429 calories
13g fat
(2g sat fat), 84mg chol, 652mg sodium, 27g carb, 1g fiber, 6g sugar, 51g protein

Before
786 calories
34g fat
(6g sat fat), 88mg chol, 1075mg sodium, 63g carb, 2g fiber, 7g sugar, 55g protein

4 SANDWICHES & SLIDERS

J-MAC'S MAPLE BBQ TURKEY SLIDERS

Serves 8

It's been exciting to see my son continue our family traditions at Masterbuilt. He's becoming a jack-of-all-trades in the office. He began in the warehouse, then moved to sales, then became a test engineer. He took on our website management before he graduated from college, then added the responsibility of leading customer service after graduation. All the while, he's also honing his cooking skills, and one of his favorite things to grill is burgers. He's learning that in order to impress your guests, you can't just grill the same ol' boring burgers. This recipe is made with spicy turkey sausage and can be served up for any meal of the day, from breakfast to dinner. It's been different to sit at his dinner table instead of our own at home, but with recipes like these, I'll be his dinner guest any day of the week!

Instructions

1. Preheat grill to 350°F (medium setting).

2. Gently mix sausage and bell pepper in a medium-sized mixing bowl. Form into 4 patties, each ½-inch thick; cover and refrigerate. Combine BBQ sauce, maple syrup, and cider vinegar. Reserve ½ cup of this sauce for basting patties on grill.

3. Remove patties from the refrigerator and grill at 350°F for 5 minutes on each side. Baste one side with sauce and grill for 5 minutes, then flip and baste other side, grilling for 5 minutes more, or until internal temperature reaches 165°F. Place bottoms and tops of buns on grill rack and cook for 2 minutes. Place burgers on the bottom half of the roll. Top each burger with ¼ cup cabbage. Serve with remaining sauce. If you like, top with a pineapple slice.

LEFT: J-Mac graduates from college

Grill

You'll need

- 1 lb. spicy turkey breakfast sausage
- 1 cup diced green bell pepper
- 1 cup of your favorite low-calorie BBQ sauce
- 2 tablespoons maple syrup
- 3 tablespoons apple cider vinegar
- 8 small whole grain rolls
- 1 cup packaged, shredded cabbage
- 4 pineapple slices, optional

4 SANDWICHES & SLIDERS

MAKE IT LIGHTER

Choosing turkey sausage instead of pork is an artery-preserving, healthier-for-the heart choice, with its lower saturated fat content.

280 calories
8g fat

(2g sat fat), 60mg chol, 989mg sodium, 35g carb, 4g fiber, 14g sugar, 18g protein

Before
724 calories
38g fat

(13g sat fat), 126mg chol, 1570mg sodium, 69g carb, 1g fiber, 30g sugar, 28g protein

Grill

You'll Need

- ¼ cup Worcestershire sauce
- ¼ cup balsamic vinegar
- 4 beef New York strip steaks (each about 1½ lbs.)
- ⅓ cup low-fat or regular mayonnaise
- ¼ cup chopped sun-dried tomatoes
- 12 whole grain bread slices
- 1 cup shredded lettuce or mixed salad greens
- 2 tomatoes, thinly sliced
- 2 tablespoons crumbled reduced-fat blue cheese

BEEF DONENESS

145°F Rare
150°F Medium-Rare
160°F Medium
165°F Medium-Well
170°F Well Done

MAKE IT LIGHTER

387 calories
11g fat
(4g sat fat), 61mg chol, 636mg sodium, 33g carb, 5g fiber, 8g sugar, 39g protein

Before
948 calories
54g fat
(26g sat fat), 265mg chol, 885mg sodium, 41g carb, 3g fiber, 7g sugar, 71g protein

BALSAMIC STRIP STEAK SANDWICHES

Serves 6

While researching the benefits of balsamic vinegar, I was pleased to learn that it's high in healthy antioxidants. The vinegar adds great flavor to this steak. My nutritionist asked me to limit red meat in my diet. These sandwiches are a great way for me to enjoy steak in a flavorful and healthier way, without sitting down to eat a giant, 16-ounce steak with baked potato.

Instructions

1. In a resealable plastic bag, combine Worcestershire sauce and balsamic vinegar. Add steaks. Seal and refrigerate, turning occasionally, for at least 30 minutes or for up to 8 hours.

2. Preheat lightly greased grill to 400°F (medium-high setting).

3. Grill steaks, with grill lid closed, over medium-high heat for 5 minutes on each side or to desired degree of doneness (see chart, left). Slice steaks across the grain into thin slices.

4. In a small bowl, combine mayonnaise and sun-dried tomatoes. Spread mayonnaise mixture on bread slices. Layer 6 bread slices with steak, lettuce, tomatoes, and blue cheese and top with remaining bread slices.

GRILLED SALMON BURGERS

Serves 8

For this recipe, a grill pan is the best tool, as the salmon is very delicate and you don't want it to fall through the grill grates. If you don't have a grill pan, heavy-duty aluminum foil will work perfectly. Make sure you use a double or triple layer of foil. You can make the patties in advance and place in the freezer for about an hour to let them set before grilling. Do not completely freeze the patties—an hour is enough!

Instructions

1. Preheat lightly greased grill to 400°F (medium-high setting).

2. In a large bowl, combine salmon, seasoning, lime pepper, and black pepper. Form mixture into 8 patties, each about ¾ inch thick. Place patties on a sheet of heavy-duty aluminum foil.

3. Place foil with patties on grill, close to the heat source. Grill with lid closed for 3 minutes on each side (do not place patties directly onto grill). Remove from grill. Serve on buns with pesto, lettuce, and tomato.

Grill

You'll Need

- 2 lbs. fresh salmon, well chopped
- 1 teaspoon "DADGUM That's Good!"™ Seasoning (page 15)
- 2 teaspoons lime pepper
- ¼ teaspoon freshly ground black pepper
- 8 whole wheat hamburger buns, split and toasted
- 2 tablespoons pesto
- Leaf lettuce
- Tomato slices

4 SANDWICHES & SLIDERS

GOOD FOR YOU

Pesto is a flavorful addition to many kinds of sandwiches. The olive oil base, pine nuts, and basil pesto ingredients are a heart-healthy switch from traditional sandwich toppings like mayonnaise.

426 calories
19g fat
(4g sat fat), 63mg chol, 476mg sodium, 34g carb, 7g fiber, 4g sugar, 30g protein

 MAINS

PORK 99

BEEF 114

POULTRY 128

FISH & SEAFOOD 158

Main dishes are the star of the meal so you don't want to sacrifice flavor when making them healthier. It's a good thing these main dishes are anything but! Enjoy tender, juicy meats prepared on the smoker or grill in a way that brings out the natural flavors and reduces the fat. You can make these mains your mealtime masterpieces.

ABOVE: Thumbs up at a trade show with Team Masterbuilt

RIGHT: Glazing a ham on set at QVC

SMOKED SAUSAGE

Serves 6   *Suggested wood chips for smoking: Hickory*

While this recipe is great served over rice, another tasty option is to serve up the sausage, peppers, and onions on a hoagie bun. You'll swear you stood in line at the State Fair for this warm, delicious sandwich.

Instructions

1. Cook brown rice according to package directions and set aside.

2. Meanwhile, preheat smoker to 250°F.

3. Place hot and mild sausage on middle rack of smoker and smoke for 1¼ hours, turning once halfway through cooking.

4. In a skillet, heat oil over medium heat. Add red and green peppers, onion, and seasoning and cook, stirring frequently, until crisp-tender, 25 to 30 minutes.

5. Remove sausage from smoker and slice into ½-inch slices. Serve over rice, and top with pepper and onion mixture.

Smoker

You'll Need

- 1 cup uncooked brown rice

- ½ lb. hot Italian sausage in casing

- 1 lb. mild Italian turkey sausage in casing

- 1 tablespoon olive oil

- 1 large red bell pepper, cut into ¼-inch strips

- 1 large green bell pepper, cut into ¼-inch strips

- 1 large sweet onion, cut into ¼-inch slices

- ½ teaspoon "DADGUM That's Good!"™ Seasoning (page 15)

MAKE IT LIGHTER

Bell peppers contain very high amounts of vitamin C and vitamin A. They also contain significant amounts of vitamin B6 and dietary fiber. They are delicious raw or cooked, and complement the pork.

495 calories
32g fat

(11g sat fat), 92mg chol, 931mg sodium, 28g carb, 2g fiber, 0g sugar, 24g protein

Before
887 calories
62g fat

(22g sat fat), 141mg chol, 2280mg sodium, 46g carb, 2g fiber, 1g sugar, 35g protein

5 MAINS PORK

SMOKED BABY BACK RIBS WITH ESPRESSO BBQ SAUCE

Serves 6   *Suggested wood chips for smoking: Mesquite or Hickory*

Yes, you read that correctly. Espresso BBQ sauce. To say that espresso is an uncommon ingredient for BBQ sauce is an understatement. In fact, we've downright puzzled a few people with this recipe. They just can't seem to comprehend how coffee ribs would taste! Once they trust us enough to taste them, they comment how this is the best BBQ sauce they've ever tasted! It's a unique flavor that will have you coming back for more, and more, and more.

Instructions

1. Season ribs with salt and pepper and smoke for 3 hours at 225°F, in preheated smoker. Use hickory chips during the first 2 hours.

2. After 3 hours, remove ribs, baste generously with espresso BBQ sauce and wrap in heavy-duty aluminum foil. Return to smoker and cook for an additional 1 to 1½ hours, or until internal temperature reaches 160°F.

Optional: During the last 10 minutes, remove ribs from the foil and baste again; place them back in the smoker, directly onto the rack, allowing the ribs to caramelize. Transfer to cutting board, cut, and serve hot.

Espresso BBQ Sauce: In a medium saucepan, combine olive oil and garlic and sauté on medium heat until golden. Remove from heat and let the garlic cool in the oil. Whisk in the ketchup, honey, vinegar, soy sauce, and espresso. Return to heat and simmer for about 15 minutes to blend flavors. Remove from heat.

Smoker

You'll Need

- 6 lbs. (3 racks) pork baby back ribs
- ¼ teaspoon sea salt
- ¼ teaspoon freshly ground black pepper

Espresso BBQ Sauce:

- 2 tablespoons extra-virgin olive oil
- 2 tablespoons minced garlic
- 1 cup low-sodium ketchup
- 1 cup honey
- ½ cup balsamic vinegar
- ¼ cup low-sodium soy sauce
- ¼ cup Starbucks® double shot espresso or strong home-brewed coffee

ALL-TIME FAVORITE

Everyone loves ribs—and these are amazing! But keep things in healthy perspective by eating a smaller portion of ribs and serving with a large tomato-topped, leafy-green salad with a vinaigrette dressing.

**687 calories
38g fat**

(12g sat fat), 219mg chol, 482mg sodium, 29g carb, 0g fiber, 26g sugar, 57g protein

5 MAINS PORK

REDNECK RIBS

Serves 8   *Suggested wood chips for smoking: Hickory*

Where I'm from, folks who like to hunt, fish, ride 4-wheelers in the mud and drive big trucks are called rednecks. One other thing rednecks love is any food that doesn't require utensils. These ribs fit the bill. They are cooked in aluminum foil and no forks are required. In fact, the only thing you'll need on the side of these ribs is a large roll of paper towels!

Instructions

1. Preheat smoker to 225°F.

2. In a medium bowl, mix pepper, onion powder, and garlic powder. Rub mixture on the ribs. Place ribs on middle rack in smoker and smoke for 1 hour. Remove ribs and baste with BBQ sauce. Double-wrap in heavy-duty aluminum foil and return to smoker. Smoke for another 2 hours or until internal temperature reaches 165°F. Then remove and baste with more sauce and serve.

BBQ Sauce: In a small saucepan over medium heat, combine ketchup, apricot jelly, steak sauce, and brown sugar and heat until well blended. Set aside.

ABOVE: 4-wheeling with the family

Smoker

You'll Need

- 4 lbs. country-style pork ribs (sliced with bone-in)
- 1 teaspoon freshly ground black pepper
- ½ teaspoon onion powder
- ½ teaspoon garlic powder

BBQ Sauce:

- 1 cup low-sodium ketchup
- ¾ cup low-sugar apricot jelly
- ½ cup steak sauce
- ¼ cup packed brown sugar

5 MAINS PORK

MAKE IT LIGHTER
431 calories
21g fat

(7g sat fat), 132mg chol, 382mg sodium, 25g carb, 0g fiber, 21g sugar, 34g protein

Before
543 calories
28g fat

(9g sat fat), 175mg chol, 943mg sodium, 25g carb, 0g fiber, 23g sugar, 45g protein

HONEY-GARLIC PORK TENDERLOINS

Serves 6

This recipe calls for grilling the tenderloins directly on the grill rack. A more forgiving method is to wrap them in foil. If wrapping, make a "boat" with heavy-duty aluminum foil. Stack three sheets of aluminum foil together, place the tenderloins in the middle of the foil and gather both of the long ends at the top. Roll these ends down toward the tenderloins together. Fold up the sides and seal tightly. By using this method (instead of simply rolling the tenderloins in foil), you contain the juices and avoid spilling them when you remove it from the foil.

Instructions

1. In a medium bowl, whisk together garlic, soy sauce, hot sauce, honey, Worcestershire sauce, and pepper.

2. Place tenderloins in a large resealable plastic bag. Pour in marinade and refrigerate, turning occasionally, for 1 hour or for up to 8 hours.

3. Preheat lightly greased grill to 400°F (medium-high setting).

4. Remove pork from marinade, discarding marinade. Grill, with grill lid closed, turning every 2 minutes, for 20 minutes. Cook for an additional 10 minutes, turning halfway through cooking or until thermometer registers 160°F at thickest point and tenderloin is slightly pink in center.

5. Place pork on a cutting board. Loosely cover with foil and let stand for 10 minutes. Cut into slices.

Grill

You'll Need

- 2 garlic cloves, minced
- ⅓ cup regular or low-sodium soy sauce
- 1 tablespoon hot sauce
- 1 tablespoon honey
- 2 teaspoons Worcestershire sauce
- ¼ teaspoon freshly ground, black pepper
- 2 pork tenderloins or 1 large, trimmed (about 2½ lbs.)

GOOD FOR YOU

Pork tenderloin can be considered "the other white meat." Comparing 3 ounces of pork tenderloin to 3 ounces of chicken breast, you may be surprised to learn that pork is lower in calories and has an almost identical amount of fat to chicken.

**225 calories
7g fat**

(2g sat fat), 120mg chol, 179mg sodium, 0g carb, 0g fiber, 0g sugar, 39g protein

5
MAINS
PORK

Grill

You'll Need

- 1 teaspoon chili powder
- 1 teaspoon ground cumin
- $\frac{1}{8}$ teaspoon cayenne pepper
- 1$\frac{1}{4}$ lbs. beef flat iron steak
- $\frac{1}{2}$ cup fresh lime juice
- 4 (8-inch) whole wheat flour tortillas, warmed
- 1 cup shredded lettuce
- 2 medium tomatoes, chopped (about 1 cup)
- $\frac{1}{4}$ cup shredded Cheddar cheese
- Salsa (optional)

GOOD FOR YOU

Flat iron steak (supposedly named because it looks like an old fashioned metal flat iron) is uniform in thickness and rectangular in shape.
Like any non-loin steak, the flat iron is best when marinated and remains most tender if it isn't cooked too well beyond medium.

**416 calories
20g fat**

(9g sat fat), 100mg chol, 473mg sodium, 28g carb, 4g fiber, 3g sugar, 33g protein

FLAT IRON STEAK TACOS

Serves 4

These tacos are delicious on their own, but I love to pair them with Alicia's Guacamole (page 33). When Alicia and her husband Gary come over for dinner we make the tacos and they bring the guac. I have to admit, when that guac comes into the kitchen, I struggle with portion control!

Instructions

1. In a small bowl, combine chili powder, cumin, and cayenne pepper. Drizzle steak with lime juice. Rub spice mixture into steak and place in a large resealable plastic bag. Seal and refrigerate, turning occasionally, for at least 2 hours or for up to 8 hours.

2. Preheat lightly greased grill to 400°F (medium-high setting).

3. Grill steak, with grill lid closed, for 5 minutes on each side or until desired degree of doneness (5 to 6 minutes per side for medium, 6 to 7 minutes per side for medium-well, 7 to 8 minutes per side for well-done). Remove steak from grill. Let stand for 5 minutes, resting in juices. Cut steak diagonally across the grain into thin slices. Serve in tortillas with lettuce, tomatoes, cheese, and desired toppings.

ABOVE: Alicia, Gary, Abigail, and J-Mac sharing a meal at our home

You'll Need

- 1½ cups green bell pepper, finely chopped
- 2 cups onion, finely chopped
- 1 teaspoon minced garlic
- 1 tablespoon extra-virgin olive oil
- 2 lbs. lean ground beef
- 1 lb. fresh Italian turkey sausage, removed from casing and crumbled
- 1 cup low-sodium BBQ sauce
- 1 cup fresh bread crumbs
- 2 large eggs, lightly beaten
- ½ teaspoon salt
- ½ teaspoon black pepper
- ¼ teaspoon cayenne pepper
- 1 cup low-sodium ketchup

SMOKED MEATLOAF

Serves 8 *Suggested wood chips for smoking: Hickory or Mesquite*

Forming the meatloaf mixture into smaller loaves ensures a more even, all–around smoke. Lightly brushing the top of the meatloaf with ketchup gives it an attractive glaze. Make sure you smoke it at 250°F. You need to get your meat to a safe internal temperature of 160°F as quickly as possible.

Instructions

1. Load the wood tray with one small handful of wood chips and preheat the smoker to 250°F.

2. In a medium skillet, sauté the green peppers, onions, garlic, and olive oil until peppers are soft. Remove from heat and pour into a large mixing bowl. Add ground round, sausage, BBQ sauce, bread crumbs, eggs, salt, pepper, and cayenne pepper; mix thoroughly.

3. Form the meat mixture into four small loaves. Place the loaves into two 11x7-inch baking pans lined with foil, 2 small loaves to a pan. Place pans on middle rack and smoke for 2 hours, making sure the internal temperature reaches 160°F.

4. Lightly brush the top of each meatloaf with ketchup 30 minutes before you remove them from the smoker. Allow the meatloaf to rest at least 15 minutes before serving.

MAKE IT LIGHTER

501 calories
26g fat
(9g sat fat), 181mg chol, 800mg sodium, 27g carb, 1g fiber, 13g sugar, 38g protein

Before
743 calories
37g fat
(12g sat fat), 274mg chol, 1101mg sodium, 37g carb, 2g fiber, 17g sugar, 64g protein

CINNAMON SIRLOIN

Serves 4

The pepper and cinnamon rub on these steaks give them a unique flavor. Want a more intense pepper flavor? Crush your own black peppercorns and use the larger pieces of pepper in the rub. Place the peppercorns inside of a clean kitchen towel and press down on them with a large spoon. This method gives you more control than a pepper grinder. Make sure you don't use these larger pieces of pepper for those with a sensitive palate, or they'll get an unwelcome pepper surprise!

Instructions

1. Preheat grill to 350°F (medium setting).

2. Allow steaks to stand at room temperature at least 15 minutes before cooking. Sprinkle both sides of steaks with salt, pepper, and cinnamon.

3. Grill steaks for 5 minutes on each side, or until internal temperature reaches 145°F. Remove steaks from grill; drizzle with 1 tablespoon of melted butter and wrap in aluminum foil. Let steaks rest for 5 minutes before serving.

Sauce: Mix butter, cinnamon, pepper, milk, and shallots in small saucepan. Bring to a simmer, stirring well. Serve with steaks as a sauce.

Grill

You'll Need

- 4 (6 ounces each) beef sirloin steaks, 1-inch thick
- ½ teaspoon salt
- 1 tablespoon black pepper
- ½ teaspoon ground cinnamon
- 1 tablespoon butter, melted

Sauce:

- 2 teaspoons butter
- Pinch of ground cinnamon
- Pinch black pepper
- ⅔ cup 2% milk
- 4 tablespoons shallots, finely chopped

MAKE IT LIGHTER

393 calories
24g fat

(11g sat fat), 85mg chol, 407mg sodium, 4g carb, 0g fiber, 2g sugar, 37g protein

Before
638 calories
47g fat

(24g sat fat), 139mg chol, 719mg sodium, 3g carb, 0g fiber, 0g sugar, 48g protein

5 MAINS BEEF

117

You'll Need

- 1 tablespoon smoked paprika
- 1 tablespoon dark brown sugar
- ½ teaspoon sea salt
- ½ teaspoon freshly ground black pepper
- 2 tablespoons olive oil
- 4 (½-inch thick) rib-eye steaks (about 2 lbs.)
- Honey barbecue sauce (optional)

BEEF DONENESS

145°F Rare
150°F Medium-Rare
160°F Medium
165°F Medium-Well
170°F Well Done

ALL-TIME FAVORITE

For a healthy alternative to an entire steak, remove the fat and slice into strips. Serve on pieces of flatbread with lettuce and tomato.

398 calories
21g fat
(8g sat fat), 134mg chol, 435mg sodium, 3g carb, 0g fiber, 3g sugar, 46g protein

GRILLED STEAKS WITH SMOKED PAPRIKA

Serves 4

If you're planning to grill steaks, but you still want some smoked flavor, this recipe gives you the best of both worlds. When you open the jar of smoked paprika, you can instantly smell the smoke aroma.

Instructions

1. Preheat lightly greased grill to 400°F (medium-high setting). In a small bowl, combine paprika, brown sugar, sea salt, and pepper. Add olive oil, mixing well. Rub paprika mixture over steaks.

2. Grill steaks, with grill lid closed, for 3 to 4 minutes per side or until desired degree of doneness. See doneness chart, left, for temperatures. Serve with honey barbecue sauce, if desired.

DADGUM GOOD BRISKET

Serves 8   *Suggested wood chips for smoking: Hickory*

One of the ways we promote our brand at Masterbuilt is with satellite media tours (SMT). In about a 3-hour period of time we do approximately 30 live television cooking segments via satellite. This Dadgum Good Brisket was the star of the show for one of these recent SMT events. Folks from all over the country tuned in to find out how to cook this juicy brisket. It was a great recipe to demonstrate on live television because it was not only dadgum good, it was dadgum easy to make!

Instructions

1. Preheat smoker to 250°F.

2. Coat beef brisket evenly with Dry Rub mixture, refrigerating extra rub to use later. Place brisket on middle rack of smoker and smoke for 3 to 5 hours or until internal temperature reaches 180°F. Check internal temperature halfway through smoking.

Dry Rub: In a medium bowl, combine paprika, garlic powder, onion powder, oregano, salt, black pepper, and cayenne pepper.

RIGHT: Slicing into a brisket during our Satellite Media Tour

Smoker

You'll Need

▶ 1 beef brisket (about 5 lbs.)

Dry Rub:

▶ ¼ cup paprika

▶ 2 tablespoons garlic powder

▶ 2 tablespoons onion powder

▶ 2½ tablespoons dried oregano

▶ 1 tablespoon kosher salt

▶ 1 tablespoon freshly ground black pepper

▶ 1 tablespoon cayenne pepper

MAKE IT LIGHTER

366 calories
12g fat
(4g sat fat), 122mg chol, 576mg sodium, 0g carb, 0g fiber, 0g sugar, 61g protein

Before
463 calories
15g fat
(6g sat fat), 163mg chol, 1252mg sodium, 0g carb, 0g fiber, 0g sugar, 82g protein

5 MAINS BEEF

ABOVE: It's Smokin' Time on Fox!
RIGHT: Gov. Huckabee slicing some tenderloin in NYC

GOVERNOR HUCKABEE'S SMOKED TENDERLOIN

Serves 12   *Suggested wood chips for smoking: Apple or Hickory*

I've known Governor Huckabee since 2008, and he's become a great friend. He's the very definition of a public servant and he loves our country. It's always fun to sit and talk with him when I visit Fox News in NYC. We've smoked his recipe at their studios and served the whole crew. I look forward to bringing this "Good For You" recipe back to Fox and the *The Huckabee Show* crew so they can enjoy it once again.

Instructions

1. Remove the fat "chain," and all membrane and silver skin from tenderloin. (You can also ask your butcher to do this for you.)

2. Fold thin end of tenderloin under so thickness is even, then tie with butcher's string in 6 to 8 places.

3. Sprinkle tenderloin with kosher salt. Wrap in plastic wrap or foil and let stand at room temperature for 1 hour. Remove plastic wrap and apply a thin coat of olive oil and sprinkle with freshly cracked black peppercorns.

4. Preheat smoker to 225°F to 250°F. Place tenderloin in smoker and smoke for 55 to 65 minutes or until the internal temperature registers 145°F or to desired doneness. Cooking times can vary a lot and this is an expensive piece of meat! Don't go by time—use a meat temperature probe and trust it more than the clock.

5. After the tenderloin has smoked to desired temperature and doneness, an option worth doing is to sear tenderloin on all four sides. Place on a very hot grill for about 2 minutes per side. This will give the outside a slight caramelized crust. I know that most of the time with beef (such as steaks) you sear it first, then cook it. Do the opposite with the tenderloin; smoke it first and THEN sear it at the end.

6. Cover loosely with foil and let rest for 10 minutes before slicing. This is when you DO want to use the clock! Don't rush it! Let those dadgum good juices settle before you go slicing into it.

Smoker

You'll Need

- 1 whole beef tenderloin (4 to 6 lbs.)
- 2 teaspoons kosher salt
- Extra-virgin olive oil to coat (about 2 tablespoons)
- 2 teaspoons freshly cracked black peppercorns

GOOD FOR YOU

Beef tenderloin is an elegant cut of meat that does not require much additional fuss. Smoking the meat brings out the flavor of this exceptional cut of meat. The protein of beef is high quality, containing all the essential amino acids.

241 calories
11g fat

(4g sat fat), 101mg chol, 472mg sodium, 0g carb, 0g fiber, 0g sugar, 33g protein

5 MAINS BEEF

ABOVE: Tonya and I photo-bomb a prime rib at QVC.

ABOVE: The crew loves our leftovers at QVC.

SMOKED PRIME RIB

Serves 6   *Suggested wood chips for smoking: Pecan*

I've been appearing on QVC with our Masterbuilt products for almost 20 years. One of the things I love the most about appearing on QVC actually happens when my live airings are finished. Waiting in the wings, just off-set, are crew members with plates in hand. They wait for the cameras to stop rolling and stand in line to enjoy the dadgum good food we pull from the smokers, grills, or turkey fryers. On smoking days, the Smoked Prime Rib is the star of the after-show.

Instructions

1. Place prime rib in a large pan. In a small bowl, combine all dry ingredients and mix well. Season roast with the mixture; let stand for 30 to 45 minutes. Load the wood tray with one small handful of wood chips and preheat the smoker to 250°F.

2. Place roast, fat side up, directly on rack in smoker. Reduce temperature to 225°F and add more wood chips. Add extra wood chips every 1 to 1½ hours during cooking time.

3. Using meat thermometer to check temperature, cook until desired temperature is reached. (See doneness chart, page 118.) Remember, meat will continue to cook for a few minutes when taken out of the smoker and covered with aluminum foil.

4. Once you have removed the prime rib, cover it with foil and let it rest for 15 to 20 minutes before cutting. This will help keep prime rib warm and juicy.

Smoker

You'll Need

- 1 (4 to 6 lbs.) beef prime rib roast
- ½ tablespoon onion powder
- ⅛ tablespoon garlic powder
- 1 tablespoon black pepper
- 1 tablespoon white pepper
- 1 tablespoon paprika
- 1 tablespoon red pepper
- 1½ teaspoons kosher salt

HEALTHY ALTERNATIVE
PRIME-RIB HERB SALAD

You don't need a huge piece of meat to enjoy the delicious flavor that prime rib offers. Top a fresh herb green salad with strips of prime rib and then top with some croutons and blue cheese crumbles.

271 calories
20g fat

(8g sat fat), 59mg chol, 262mg sodium, 6g carb, 1g fiber, 3g sugar, 18g protein

Recipe based on: 1 cup herb salad greens, 2 T. chopped heirloom tomatoes, 5 croutons, 4 small strips of cooked prime rib (about 3 oz.), 1 T. fat-free Italian Dressing, 1 T. low-fat, reduced-sodium blue cheese crumbles. (Serves 1)

ALL-TIME FAVORITE

"Prime Rib" is not a specific cut of beef but is actually a preparation method for a beef rib roast. I don't recommend well done for a prime rib. For medium rare to medium, the cooking time is approximately 4 to 6 hours—1 hour per pound.

627 calories
51g fat

(21g sat fat), 156mg chol, 640mg sodium, 0g carb, 0g fiber, 0g sugar, 42g protein

5 MAINS BEEF

When you're selecting steaks, you have the option of choosing a lower cost cut. A filet is more of a splurge, but when it comes to my daughters, I don't mind. Steak is one of Brooke's favorite foods. We will soon be choosing a very important menu with her. In fact, her most important menu ever— her wedding menu! You can be sure steak will be on her wish list.

TOP CENTER: Brooke slicing some filets at QVC
ABOVE: Brooke with her fiancé Brian
RIGHT: At *Fox and Friends* on the "curvy couch" with Brooke and Brian

BROOKE'S SMOKED BEEF FILET STEAKS

Serves 6

Suggested wood chips for smoking: Hickory

Instructions

1. In a medium bowl, combine Heinz 57 Sauce, A.1. Steak Sauce, olive oil, red wine vinegar, Worcestershire sauce, onion powder, minced garlic, garlic salt, and pepper to taste, mixing well. Place steaks in a resealable plastic bag. Pour marinade over steaks, seal, and refrigerate. Marinate, turning occasionally, for at least 4 hours or overnight.

2. Preheat smoker to 225°F.

3. Place steaks on lower rack of smoker and smoke for 35 to 40 minutes or until internal temperature reaches desired doneness. See chart, page 118.

Smoker

You'll Need

- ¼ cup Heinz 57 Sauce
- 2 tablespoons A.1. Steak Sauce
- 1 tablespoon extra-virgin olive oil
- 2 tablespoons red wine vinegar
- 1 tablespoon Worcestershire sauce
- 1 teaspoon onion powder
- 2 teaspoons minced garlic
- ¼ teaspoon garlic salt
- Freshly ground black pepper
- 6 beef filet steaks (each 1-inch thick)

5 MAINS BEEF

MAKE IT LIGHTER

245 calories
13g fat
(4g sat fat), 78mg chol, 375mg sodium, 5g carb, 0g fiber, 4g sugar, 26g protein

Before
273 calories
15g fat
(5g sat fat), 78mg chol, 742mg sodium, 6g carb, 0g fiber, 4g sugar, 26g protein

CENTER: Chef Loryn
RIGHT: Our pastor Dr. Bill Purvis and his wife Debbie
BELOW: Loryn and BJ with their son Kellan

LORYN'S SALSA VERDE SKIRT STEAK AND GRILLED GREEN BEAN SALAD

Serves 8

Loryn Purvis is the daughter-in-law of my pastor and his wife, Dr. Bill and Debbie Purvis. The Purvis family are great friends and although we are all very busy, it's so nice when we can get together and share a meal. They have continually raved about Loryn's cooking at family events. She is a graduate of the San Diego Culinary Institute and she founded MenuTherapy.com, an online meal planning service. This recipe comes from one of her healthy meal plans. For busy, on-the-go families, this is such a helpful service. Be sure to check out Loryn's site and enjoy her recipes with your own family.

Instructions:

Steak/Salsa Verde:

1. Mix ¼ cup oil, garlic, and lemon zest in a medium bowl. Let marinate for 20 minutes. Add all herbs to oil mixture; stir until well coated. Let stand until herbs begin to wilt, about 10 minutes. Stir in remaining ¼ cup oil, then red wine vinegar. Season salsa verde with salt and pepper.

2. Heat grill to high heat. Season skirt steak with salt and pepper to taste and grill until charred, 2 minutes per side for medium-rare. Transfer steak to a serving platter; let rest for 5 minutes, allowing juices to accumulate on the platter. Transfer skirt steak to a cutting board; slice against the grain on a diagonal.

3. Return the steak to the platter with its juices. Spoon half of herb salsa verde over steaks. Pass remaining herb salsa verde alongside when serving.

Green Bean Salad:

1. Toss green beans with 1 tablespoon of olive oil and salt to taste. Place a grill basket on a grill heated to high heat. Add green beans and lower temperature to medium-high. Toss the beans every minute or so and continue cooking until beans begin to char and the skin is blistering. Remove from heat.

2. To make the Mustard Vinaigrette, combine Dijon mustard, red wine vinegar, dill weed, and honey. Slowly drizzle in the olive oil and whisk quickly to combine. Season to taste with salt and pepper.

3. In a serving dish, combine the green beans, cherry tomatoes, and mustard vinaigrette. Toss to coat and serve alongside the skirt steak.

Grill

You'll Need:

Steak/Salsa Verde:

- 2 lbs. beef skirt steak, trimmed
- ½ cup extra-virgin olive oil, divided
- 4 garlic cloves, minced
- Zest of 1 lemon
- 1 cup flat leaf parsley, minced
- 1 cup arugula, minced
- ¼ cup basil, minced
- ¼ cup fresh mint, minced
- ¼ cup red wine vinegar
- ½ teaspoon salt
- ½ teaspoon black pepper

Green Bean Salad/Mustard Vinaigrette:

- 1 lb. green beans
- 2 tablespoons Dijon mustard
- 2 tablespoons red wine vinegar
- 1 tablespoon dill weed
- 1 tablespoon honey
- ½ cup extra-virgin olive oil
- 1 cup cherry tomatoes, halved

5 MAINS BEEF

GOOD FOR YOU

381 calories
26g fat
(steak and salad)
(7g sat fat), 67mg chol, 223mg sodium, 7g carb, 2g fiber, 4g sugar, 31g protein

Grill

You'll Need

- 4 boneless skinless chicken breasts (about 1¼ lbs.)

Barbecue Sauce:

- 1½ cups apple cider vinegar
- 1 cup low-sodium ketchup
- 1 cup chili sauce
- 2 tablespoons Worcestershire sauce
- 2 garlic cloves, minced
- ¼ teaspoon cayenne pepper

GOOD FOR YOU

You can also use bone-in chicken, which gets more tender results, but grill for 15 to 20 minutes longer or until internal temperature reaches 165°F.

184 calories
3g fat
(0g sat fat), 100mg chol, 298mg sodium, 6g carb, 0g fiber, 2g sugar, 32g protein

CLASSIC BARBECUE CHICKEN

Serves 4

BBQ is such a regional dish. The region you grew up in usually determines your preferred sauce. Because I travel so much, I've learned to appreciate all types and flavors of BBQ. This sauce marries the flavors of vinegar and ketchup, with a bit of a kick from the cayenne pepper.

Instructions

1. Place chicken in a large resealable plastic bag or shallow dish. Pour 1 cup of barbecue sauce over chicken and coat both sides. Cover and refrigerate for at least 30 minutes or for up to 2 hours. Reserve remaining sauce for later use.

2. Preheat lightly greased grill to 400°F (medium-high setting). Remove chicken from Barbecue Sauce, discarding sauce. Grill chicken, with grill lid closed, for 20 to 35 minutes, turning every 4 minutes, until chicken is no longer pink inside and internal temperature reaches 165°F (cooking time will vary depending on size of chicken and whether bone-in or out). Brush chicken with 1 cup of reserved sauce during last 1 to 2 minutes of cooking. Let stand for 5 minutes. Serve with remaining 1½ cups of reserved barbecue sauce.

Barbecue Sauce: In a medium saucepan over medium heat, combine vinegar, ketchup, chili sauce, Worcestershire sauce, garlic, and cayenne pepper. Bring to a boil. Reduce heat and simmer, stirring occasionally, for 30 minutes. Let cool.

CHICKEN PESTO KABOBS

Serves 6

When making kabobs, it can be frustrating when the food spins on the skewer. If you have a problem with that, try using two skewers on each kabob. These secure the food and allow you to pick up the entire kabob and flip it over without the food spinning. Remember to always soak wood skewers in water for at least 30 minutes before grilling, so they don't burn.

Instructions

1. Preheat grill to 325°F grill (medium setting).

2. Place fresh basil, garlic, pine nuts, black pepper, kosher salt, extra-virgin olive oil, and cheese in a food processor or blender. Process to make a pesto. Add additional olive oil to "thin out" if needed. Set aside.

3. Soak wood skewers in water for 30 minutes. Sprinkle chicken tenders with salt and pepper. Cut into 1 inch chunks. Make kabobs with chicken chunks, cherry tomatoes, and mushrooms. Coat chicken and veggies generously with the pesto sauce.

4. Grill kabobs for 4 to 5 minutes on each side. Serve immediately.

Grill

You'll Need

- ▸ 1 cup firmly-packed fresh basil
- ▸ 1 garlic clove
- ▸ 1½ tablespoons pine nuts
- ▸ ½ teaspoon coarse black pepper
- ▸ ½ teaspoon kosher salt
- ▸ Approximately 2 tablespoons extra-virgin olive oil
- ▸ ½ cup grated pecorino or Parmesan cheese
- ▸ 1½ lbs. boneless, skinless chicken tenders
- ▸ ¼ teaspoon salt
- ▸ ¼ teaspoon black pepper
- ▸ 18 cherry tomatoes
- ▸ 18 fresh whole mushrooms
- ▸ 6 (9-inch) wooden skewers

GOOD FOR YOU

Kabobs originated in the Middle East as pieces of lamb cooked on skewers. Today, however, kabobs are made with a variety of meats, vegetables, and fruits.

222 calories
10g fat

(1g sat fat), 83mg chol, 367mg sodium, 5g carb, 1g fiber, 0g sugar, 28g protein

RIGHT: The family enjoying pizza before Tonya's "Lean" recipe!

TONYA'S LEAN GREEN PIZZA

Serves 8

My wife Tonya and I travel often and one of our go-to favorites is pizza. As much as we love extra-cheesy, meaty pizza, we know that this recipe had to undergo a healthy makeover, too. This pesto makes a great alternative sauce, and the grilled chicken is a yummy way to pack protein onto each slice. Tonya loves using our electric patio grill to make these pizzas!

Instructions

1. Place fresh basil, garlic, pine nuts, black pepper, kosher salt, extra-virgin olive oil, and cheese in a food processor or blender. Process to make a pesto. Add additional olive oil to "thin out" if needed. Set aside.

2. Combine marjoram, dried basil, oregano, thyme, and garlic powder to make dry seasoning blend. Sprinkle chicken tenders with pepper. Coat with dry seasoning blend on both sides. Grill for 4 to 5 minutes on each side on a 325°F grill (medium setting).

3. Spread pesto sauce on pizza crust. Slice chicken tenders and place on top of pesto, spreading evenly across the crust. Sprinkle entire pizza with reduced-fat cheese.

4. Grill pizza on a stone or grill pan for 10 minutes at 300°F. Garnish with fresh basil if desired. Slice and serve.

LEFT: Bailey baked up some mini-pizzas.

Grill

You'll Need

- 1 cup firmly-packed fresh basil
- 1 garlic clove
- 1½ tablespoons pine nuts
- ½ teaspoon coarse black pepper
- ½ teaspoon kosher salt
- 2 tablespoons extra-virgin olive oil
- ½ cup grated pecorino or Parmesan cheese
- 1 teaspoon *each* dried marjoram, basil, oregano, and thyme
- ½ teaspoon garlic powder
- 1½ lbs. boneless skinless chicken tenders
- ½ teaspoon pepper
- 1 large whole wheat thin pizza crust
- 1½ cups reduced-fat Italian shredded cheese blend

5 MAINS POULTRY

GOOD FOR YOU

Besides being delicious, basil has been used for centuries to treat arthritis and to speed wound healing.

388 calories
13g fat
(4g sat fat), 63mg chol, 714mg sodium, 31g carb, 0g fiber, 1g sugar, 34g protein

ABOVE: Bailey making chicken fingers for the family
RIGHT: 5K run with Bailey and family

BAILEY'S CHICKEN FINGERS WITH HONEY MUSTARD

Serves 4

My entire family has been very supportive of my healthier eating choices. My daughter Bailey took that up another level and decided to set some weight loss goals of her own. We've been encouragers to one another and I'm proud of the hard work she's put in. She, her sister, and Tonya joined a local gym and they've been finding ways to enjoy some of their favorites in healthy ways. These chicken fingers are an all-time favorite at our house, so now we serve them sliced atop fresh fruit and leafy greens.

Instructions

1. Fill deep fryer halfway with oil and heat to 350°F.

2. In a medium shallow dish, combine egg and buttermilk. In another bowl, combine crackers, bread crumbs, and pepper. Dip chicken in egg mixture and then dredge in bread crumb mixture.

3. Fry chicken in batches, turning as needed, for 3 to 4 minutes or until golden brown. Use a metal slotted spoon to transfer to paper towels to drain. Serve immediately with honey-mustard mixture.

Honey-Mustard Sauce: In a small bowl, combine Dijon mustard and honey, stirring well. Set aside.

Fryer

You'll Need

- 1 gallon cooking oil
- 1 egg, lightly beaten
- ½ cup buttermilk
- 1 cup crushed crackers (about 20), such as saltines
- 1 cup seasoned bread crumbs
- ½ teaspoon freshly ground black pepper
- 1¼ lbs. boneless chicken tenders (about 8 small pieces)

Honey-Mustard Sauce:

- ½ cup Dijon mustard
- 6 tablespoons honey

HEALTHY ALTERNATIVE

FRESH FRUIT AND CHICKEN SALAD

Eating smaller portions of an all-time favorite is a start to eating healthy. Slice a chicken finger on top of fresh fruit and greens for a refreshing salad.

**367 calories
15g fat**

(1g sat fat), 62mg chol, 536mg sodium, 38g carb, 6g fiber, 16g sugar, 20g protein

Recipe based on 1 fried chicken tender, 3 strawberries, 1 kiwi, ¼ cup blueberries, 3 lettuce leaves. (Serves 1)

ALL-TIME FAVORITE

These crunchy, lightly breaded chicken fingers are a treat for sure! Just eat one atop a salad and you'll cut the calories and still enjoy the great taste.

**575 calories
30g fat**

(2g sat fat), 123mg chol, 979mg sodium, 37g carb, 1g fiber, 9g sugar, 36g protein

CARIBBEAN KABOBS

Serves 6

We had a great year at Masterbuilt in 2013. I challenged our team to meet certain goals and they surpassed them. As a reward for all of their efforts, I surprised them with a cruise to the Bahamas! We had four days of relaxing and eating, and these kabobs remind me of those Caribbean flavors! Being successful is rewarding, but being able to share in that with my entire team was the biggest reward of all.

Instructions

Marinade: In a non-reactive bowl, combine puréed mango, lime juice, shallots, brown sugar, olive oil, curry powder, garlic paste, cayenne pepper, and salt. Add chicken pieces, toss well to coat, and refrigerate 8 hours, or overnight.

1. Preheat grill to 300°F (low to medium heat).

2. Drain marinade from chicken into a small saucepan. Cook over medium heat, stirring often, for 3 to 5 minutes. Set aside for basting chicken during grilling.

3. Soak wood skewers in water for 30 minutes. Thread 4 to 5 chicken pieces onto each skewer, alternating chicken with plantains, papaya, and pineapple pieces. Grill on medium heat for 5 to 7 minutes per side, occasionally brushing kabobs with reserved marinade that has been cooked. Remove from grill and serve.

Grill

You'll Need

- 2 lbs. boneless chicken breasts, cut into 1½-inch cubes
- ½ cup green plantains, cut into 1½-inch pieces
- 4 cups papaya cut into 1½-inch pieces
- 3 cups pineapple cut into 1½-inch pieces

Marinade:

- 1 fresh mango, peeled, cored and puréed
- 3 tablespoons fresh lime juice
- 2 tablespoons shallots, finely chopped
- 2 tablespoons brown sugar, firmly packed
- 2 tablespoons extra-virgin olive oil
- 1 tablespoon curry powder
- 1 tablespoon garlic paste
- ½ teaspoon cayenne pepper
- ½ teaspoon salt
- 6 (9-inch) wooden skewers

GOOD FOR YOU

Grilling fruits with chicken is a great combination—and good for you! Like bananas, plantains are a good source of potassium and fiber. Papaya and pineapple are good sources of vitamin A and vitamin C.

179 calories
4g fat
(0g sat fat), 27mg chol, 150mg sodium, 30g carb, 4g fiber, 21g sugar, 10g protein

You'll Need

- 1 whole fresh chicken, 4 to 5 lbs.

- 1 head cabbage

- 2 large yellow squash, sliced

- 1 lb. carrots, sliced

- 1 tablespoon plus one teaspoon Italian seasoning, separated

STEAMED WHOLE CHICKEN AND VEGGIES

Serves 6

When I mention that I'm going to steam a recipe in my indoor turkey fryer I normally get puzzled looks and, "Huh?" People are always surprised to learn that you can put water in our turkey fryer instead of oil and cook up some healthy meals.

Instructions

1. Fill your Butterball® Indoor Electric Turkey Fryer with water to the MAX line. Set to 375°F. Place basket on drain clips.

2. Remove the giblets and any clips from the chicken. Once water is boiling, place whole chicken in basket (leave basket on drain clips; do not put down into water). Set a timer for 1 hour and 10 minutes.

3. Peel and chop cabbage. Add to the basket with the chicken when there is 40 minutes left on the timer. Sprinkle 1 tablespoon Italian seasoning over chicken and cabbage.

4. Add the squash and carrots when there is 20 minutes left on the timer. Sprinkle 1 teaspoon Italian seasoning over chicken and veggies.

5. Once the internal temp of the chicken is 165°F, it is done. Remove and place in bowl to serve.

GOOD FOR YOU

Steamed chicken isn't the prettiest dish, but it is so delicious and good for you. The veggies add nutrition and color to the mix.

473 calories
17g fat

(5g sat fat), 202mg chol, 260mg sodium, 12g carb, 6g fiber, 1g sugar, 68g protein

TONY'S GRILLED TURKEY SKEWERS

Serves 4

While I enjoy the experiences and new food I get to try while traveling, what I enjoy most is meeting new friends. I met Chef Tony Seta at Butterball®. He is a Master Chef and it was my privilege to cook with him in the Butterball kitchens. I was in awe of his knowledge and skills and he has been so generous to share recipes with our team. Tony's a great guy and he cooks a mean turkey, which makes him not only a Master Chef, but a Masterbuilt Chef!

Instructions

1. Soak skewers in water for 30 minutes. Lightly spray each skewer with olive oil. Place turkey on skewers. Cold smoke the turkey for 35 to 40 minutes. Then refrigerate until grill time.

2. Lightly oil the grill and preheat grill to 350°F (medium heat). Cook for about 15 to 20 minutes or until turkey is 165°F on meat thermometer. Place watermelon on skewers. Flash grill the watermelon skewers on hot grill. Top skewers with blood orange segments and serve atop brown rice or herbed risotto. Drizzle with Blood Orange Vinaigrette.

Blood Orange Vinaigrette: Whisk together orange juice, olive oil, salt, and pepper.

Smoker/Grill

You'll Need

- ► Turkey tenders (about 1 lb) cut into 12 1½-inch pieces
- ► Half watermelon cut into 12 3x3-inch pieces
- ► 2 blood oranges

Blood Orange Vinaigrette:

- ► ¼ cup blood orange juice
- ► 1 tablespoon olive oil
- ► ¼ teaspoon salt
- ► ½ teaspoon black pepper
- ► 4 (9-inch) wooden skewers

GOOD FOR YOU

Blood oranges have a characteristic maroon-colored flesh that adds vibrant eye-appeal to any dish. The taste of the fruit is a strong orange flavor mixed with a hint of raspberry.

**247 calories
13g fat**

(4g sat fat), 51mg chol, 345mg sodium, 12g carb, 3g fiber, 3g sugar, 19g protein

5 MAINS POULTRY

GEORGIA PEACH HENS

Serves 2　　　　　*Suggested wood chips for smoking: Apple*

When you're from Georgia, The Peach State, you've most likely tried peaches in just about every way imaginable. Peach jam, peach cobbler, peach ice cream—you name it! Pairing those peaches with game hens isn't common, but it sure is delicious. My favorite Georgia peaches aren't in a recipe—they are right by my side!

Instructions

1. Preheat smoker to 225°F.

2. In a bowl, combine peach preserves, orange juice, cinnamon, salt, and ginger to create a glaze. Brush glaze over Cornish game hens. Place hens on middle rack of smoker; smoke hens for 3½ hours or until internal temperature reaches 165°F. Remove and let stand for 10 minutes before serving.

Smoker

You'll Need

- ⅓ cup peach preserves
- 1 tablespoon orange juice
- ¼ teaspoon ground cinnamon
- Pinch salt
- Pinch ground ginger
- 2 Cornish game hens, rinsed thoroughly and patted dry (each about 1½ lbs.)

RIGHT: Shirley and Tonya at QVC
BELOW: My Georgia girls are all smiles!

ALL-TIME FAVORITE
To save some calories, divide each hen into two servings and serve with a fruit salad.

**809 calories
48g fat**
(14g sat fat), 340mg chol, 352mg sodium, 36g carb, 0g fiber, 33g sugar, 58g protein

5 MAINS POULTRY

139

Smoker

You'll Need

- 1 whole roasting chicken, butterflied (about 4 lbs.)
- 2 tablespoons extra-virgin olive oil, divided
- ½ package Louisiana Fish Fry Gumbo Mix (5-ounce package)
- 1 cup sliced celery
- 1¾ cups sliced okra
- 2 teaspoons minced garlic
- ½ cup thinly sliced green onions, green parts only
- ½ cup chopped sweet onion
- ½ teaspoon liquid shrimp boil
- ¾ lb. turkey kielbasa sausage
- 1 cup uncooked brown rice

MAKE IT LIGHTER

Originating in southern Louisiana in the 1700s, gumbo has many variations but is often categorized by the thickener used in the recipe. In this dish, okra is the thickening agent.

451 calories
17g fat

(3g sat fat), 145mg chol, 1117mg sodium, 22g carb, 2g fiber, 2g sugar, 49g protein

Before

683 calories
39g fat

(10g sat fat), 164mg chol, 2818mg sodium, 37g carb, 4g fiber, 0g sugar, 46g protein

DADGUM GOOD GUMBO

Serves 10   *Suggested wood chips for smoking: Apple*

Gumbo is another one of those regional dishes. The ingredients will vary depending on where you're from. For us, smoked chicken makes it a good Georgia gumbo. This recipe freezes well, so I recommend doubling (or even tripling) the recipe. Simply pour into gallon-size plastic bags after it's cooled and freeze for later.

Instructions

1. Preheat smoker to 250°F. Pierce each half of the chicken with a fork. Baste each with 1 tablespoon olive oil. Place chicken on middle rack of smoker and smoke for 2 to 3½ hours or until internal temperature reaches 165°F.

2. Meanwhile, in a large stockpot, prepare gumbo mix according to package directions. Stir in celery, okra, garlic, green onions, sweet onion, and liquid shrimp boil, combining well. Bring to a boil. Reduce heat to medium-low and simmer, covered, for 15 minutes.

3. When chicken is finished cooking, let cool and pull meat from bone. Slice turkey sausage into ¼-inch slices. Add both chicken and sausage to gumbo and simmer on low for 20 minutes. Add uncooked rice, stir well, and simmer on low for another 15 minutes. If rice needs additional cooking, turn heat off, leave pot covered, and let stand until rice is ready. If you prefer the gumbo to be thinner, add a small amount of water and stir well. Serve with French bread.

LEMON PEPPER CHICKEN

Serves 6

Grilled fresh vegetables make a tasty complement to this chicken dish. I like to cut zucchini in half lengthwise, coat it in olive oil, and sprinkle with salt and pepper. Place them on the grill alongside the chicken during the last 15 minutes of the cooking time.

Instructions

1. Using poultry shears, butterfly* the chicken, open it flat, and place the breast side up in a large baking dish or pan.

2. Coarsely crush peppercorns, fennel, and cinnamon in a blender. Mix with the crushed garlic and rub over the entire chicken, inside and out. Cut the lemons into wedges and squeeze juice over the chicken. Scatter the lemon pieces under and over the chicken. Marinate the chicken in refrigerator overnight in a covered baking dish or resealable plastic bag.

3. Preheat the grill to 350°F (medium setting). Pour melted butter over chicken. With grill lid closed, grill chicken for 15 minutes, then turn and grill an additional 15 minutes, or until internal temperature reaches 165°F. Remove from grill, cover with aluminum foil, and let chicken stand for 10 minutes before carving and serving.

*Refer to page 151 for how to butterfly a chicken.

Grill

You'll Need

- ▶ 1 whole chicken (about 3½ lbs.)
- ▶ 2 tablespoons black peppercorns
- ▶ 1 tablespoon fennel seeds
- ▶ 1 cinnamon stick
- ▶ 2 garlic cloves, crushed
- ▶ 2 medium lemons, cut into wedges
- ▶ 2 tablespoons butter, melted

5 MAINS POULTRY

GOOD FOR YOU

The warm flavor of cinnamon is a welcome surprise mixed with the tangy lemon, garlic, and pepper.

377 calories
17g fat

(4g sat fat), 162mg chol, 352mg sodium, 4g carb, 0g fiber, 0g sugar, 50g protein

JAMAICAN JERK CHICKEN

Serves 12

My wife Tonya and I celebrated our 25th wedding anniversary in 2013. We renewed our vows in Jamaica, surrounded by our family and some friends. The trip was filled with fun times and lots of local food. You can't leave Jamaica without enjoying Jerk Chicken, and this recipe gives you a little taste of Jamaica at home.

Instructions

1. In a food processor or blender purée the scallions, chilies, soy sauce, lime juice, allspice, mustard, bay leaves, garlic, salt, sugar, thyme, cinnamon, and olive oil.

2. Divide thighs and place in 2 heavy-duty resealable plastic bags, about 6 per bag. Spoon the marinade over the thighs, coating them well. Press out the excess air and seal the bags. Let the thighs marinate in the refrigerator for at least 24 hours, turning the bags over several times.

3. Preheat the grill to 350°F (medium setting). Grill the thighs on medium heat, for 10 to 15 minutes on each side, or until internal temperature reaches 165°F.

ABOVE:

Our family celebrating our 25th wedding anniversary in Jamaica

Grill

You'll Need

- ▶ 2 cups scallions, chopped
- ▶ 2 habanero chiles, seeded
- ▶ 1 tablespoon low-sodium soy sauce
- ▶ 2 tablespoons fresh lime juice
- ▶ 5 teaspoons allspice, ground
- ▶ 1 tablespoon Dijon mustard
- ▶ 2 bay leaves, crumbled and center ribs discarded
- ▶ 2 garlic cloves, crushed
- ▶ 1 teaspoon salt
- ▶ 2 teaspoons sugar
- ▶ 1½ teaspoons dried thyme
- ▶ 1 teaspoon cinnamon
- ▶ 1 tablespoon extra-virgin olive oil
- ▶ 12 chicken thighs (bone-in, skin-on)

MAKE IT LIGHTER

190 calories
14g fat

(4g sat fat), 77mg chol, 224mg sodium, 2g carb, 0g fiber, 0g sugar, 16g protein

Before
380 calories
28g fat

(8g sat fat), 154mg chol, 981mg sodium, 3g carb, 0g fiber, 1g sugar, 32g protein

5 MAINS POULTRY

DADGUM GOOD SMOKED TURKEY

Serves 12   *Suggested wood chips for smoking: Apple*

When it comes to marinades and seasonings, you've got a world of choices out there. Thankfully, we have many more healthy options now. If you've got a favorite injection marinade or seasoning that works with your own healthy eating plan, use that and follow these same cooking instructions to create your own dadgum good turkey. Make sure you cook to temp and not time—the turkey is done when it reaches 165°F internal temp.

Instructions

Option 1 (shorter cook time)

1. Fill water tray ½ full with a mixture of ½ apple juice and ½ water. Preheat smoker to 275°F.

2. Rinse and dry the thawed turkey. Using a marinade injection syringe, inject turkey with Butterball Buttery Creole marinade. Season outside and inside of turkey with Butterball Cajun Seasoning, rubbing it into the skin.

3. Place turkey on middle rack in smoker and close the door. Smoke for 5½ hours or until internal temperature in breast reaches 165°F. (This total cooking time is for a 19-pound whole turkey. Based on the weight of the turkey, you will need to adjust the total cooking time. Estimated time at 275°F is about 18 minutes per pound. Make sure the internal temperature in the breast reaches 165°F.)

Option 2 (longer cook time)

1. Fill water pan ⅓ full with mixture of apple juice and water. Preheat smoker to 225°F.

2. See Step 2 above.

3. Place turkey on middle rack in smoker and close the door. Smoke for 9½ hours or until internal temperature in breast reaches 165°F. (This total cooking time is for a 19-pound whole turkey. Based on the weight of the turkey, you will need to adjust the total cooking time. Estimated time at 225°F is about 30 minutes per pound. Make sure the internal temperature in the breast reaches 165°F.)

Smoker

You'll Need

▶ 50/50 mixture of apple juice and water

▶ 1 whole turkey, fresh or completely thawed (about 19 lbs.)

▶ 16-ounce bottle Butterball® Buttery Creole Injection Marinade or your favorite marinade

▶ 1 tablespoon Butterball Cajun Seasoning or your favorite Cajun seasoning

▶ Seasonings and marinades (optional)

We highly recommend the Butterball Seasoning Kit with the Buttery Creole Marinade and the Butterball Cajun Seasoning. However, there are other options if you like a milder flavor. You can inject the turkey with chicken broth and tuck bay leaves under the skin or choose the marinade of your choice.

ALL-TIME FAVORITE

Choosing a low-sodium chicken broth to inject into the turkey will reduce the sodium but keep the flavor.

427 calories 23g fat
(7g sat fat), 169mg chol, 1583mg sodium, 0g carb, 0g fiber, 0g sugar, 55g protein

5 MAINS POULTRY

145

You'll Need

- 1 lb. boneless, skinless chicken breasts (about 4, 4-ounce pieces)
- 1 cup reduced-sodium chicken broth
- ½ cup balsamic vinegar
- ½ teaspoon garlic powder
- 1 teaspoon salt
- 1 teaspoon black pepper
- 1 tablespoon minced garlic
- ½ cup chopped green onions
- Juice of 1 lemon
- 1 tablespoon fresh (or dry) thyme

KIMBERLY'S GRILLED BALSAMIC VINEGAR CHICKEN

Serves 4

Kimberly works in our Marketing Department at Masterbuilt, and her only request when sharing her recipe for Grilled Balsamic Vinegar Chicken was that we not include her photo. She's camera-shy at Masterbuilt and goes to great measures to dodge photos. She's actually gotten pretty clever at using props to hide her face! We don't mind her hiding, as long as she doesn't hide this chicken from us!

Instructions

1. Using a covered dish, combine all ingredients, except thyme. Reserve ¼ cup for basting later. Pour remaining marinade over chicken breast. Cover dish and let chicken marinate in mixture for 30 minutes.

2. Lightly oil the cooking grill grate. Preheat the grill to 375°F (medium-high setting).

3. Remove chicken from marinade. Place chicken breasts on the grill and cook 10 to 15 minutes per side or until no longer pink and until internal temperature reaches 165°F.

4. Use reserved marinade to baste the chicken as it cooks for added flavor. Garnish cooked chicken with thyme, if desired.

GOOD FOR YOU

The simple marinade used in this recipe adds just the right amount of tangy flavors without taking away from the flavor of the chicken.

140 calories
3g fat

(1g sat fat), 60mg chol, 443mg sodium, 4g carb, 0g fiber, 3g sugar, 23g protein

CHICKEN THIGHS WITH SALSA

Serves 6

Here's one time when cheaper is actually better. Chicken thighs may be one of the cheaper cuts, but you'll find they do great on the grill. Thighs are more flavorful and the extra fat in the skin makes them better suited to grilling. Some folks like to brine their chicken, but this marinade gives it all the juice it needs to make it dadgum good.

Instructions

1. Place chicken thighs in a resealable plastic bag. Add red onion, lemon zest, ground cumin, lemon juice, and olive oil. Seal and marinate in refrigerator for 3 to 6 hours. Occasionally, turn bag to spread marinade evenly.

2. Set grill to 375°F (medium to high setting). Remove chicken from marinade; reserve for basting. Sprinkle chicken with salt and pepper. In a small saucepan, bring marinade to a boil.

3. Grill chicken for 12 minutes per side or until internal temperature reaches 165° F, basting occasionally with marinade. Remove from grill and serve with salsa.

Salsa: In a medium bowl, mix the corn, tomato, red onion, cilantro, olive oil, lemon juice, cumin, and jalapeño. Peel, pit and dice avocado. Add to salsa and season with salt and pepper.

Grill

You'll Need

- 4 lbs. chicken thighs, skin on
- ¼ cup chopped red onion
- 1 tablespoon grated lemon zest
- 1 teaspoon ground cumin
- ¼ cup fresh lemon juice
- 3 tablespoons olive oil
- ¼ teaspoon salt
- ¼ teaspoon black pepper

Salsa:

- 1 cup fresh corn kernels
- 1 large tomato, seeded and diced
- ⅔ cup chopped red onion
- ½ cup cilantro, chopped
- 2 tablespoons olive oil
- 1 tablespoon fresh lemon juice
- ½ teaspoon cumin
- 1 jalapeño, seeded and minced
- 1 avocado
- ¼ teaspoon salt
- ¼ teaspoon black pepper

5 MAINS POULTRY

GOOD FOR YOU

523 calories
40g fat

(8g sat fat), 139mg chol, 282mg sodium, 9g carb, 2g fiber, 1g sugar, 30g protein

ABOVE: We miss MeMaw, and here, Tonya and MeMaw share a quiet moment.
RIGHT: MeMaw with the kids

MEMAW'S SOUTHERN FRIED CHICKEN

Serves 6

When I first sat down with our publishing team to discuss recipes for this book, I had one condition—my momma's Southern Fried Chicken would still make the cut. I know it's an indulgence, but I don't mind. My momma was the sweetest lady I've ever known. We lost her in 2011 and we love keeping reminders of her all around us. In fact, our test kitchen at Masterbuilt is called MeMaw's Kitchen. When I was younger, I remember my mom would peel the skin off of her chicken in her own effort to eat healthier. My brothers and I would fight over the skin! 35 years of working together, that's the only thing we've ever fought over! Now, I'm afraid I have to pass the skin to someone else, too. Every once in a while, I do have to enjoy a piece and remember my momma.

Instructions

1. Fill Butterball® or Masterbuilt Fryer with oil. Heat to 375°F; this will take approximately 15 to 20 minutes.

2. Sprinkle chicken with salt and pepper. Pour the buttermilk into medium bowl. Place the flour in a separate medium-sized bowl. Dip the chicken pieces in buttermilk coating them well, then dredge in the flour.

3. Place the chicken pieces in the fryer and cook for 15 minutes until golden brown. Allow the chicken to drain in fryer basket before removing. Place on paper towels to rest.

Fryer

You'll Need

- 1 gallon cooking oil
- 1 3 lb. fryer chicken, cut into pieces
- 1 teaspoon salt
- 1 teaspoon black pepper
- 1 cup buttermilk
- 1½ cups self-rising flour

ABOVE: I loved my sweet Momma!

HEALTHY ALTERNATIVE

SLICED CHICKEN AND SALAD GREENS

Enjoy this all-time favorite chicken on a salad and save some fat and calories. Remove the skin after frying, slice the meat, and add to your favorite fresh salad greens.

**136 calories
4g fat**

(1g sat fat), 25mg chol, 220mg sodium, 7g carb, 2g fiber, 1g sugar, 18g protein

Recipe based on ½ cup sliced chicken without skin, 1½ cups salad greens, 2 T. shredded carrots, 2 cherry tomatoes, 1 T. fat-free ranch dressing. (Serves 1)

ALL-TIME FAVORITE

Enjoy this delightful recipe with green vegetables and a fresh fruit salad to make a complete meal.

**787 calories
45g fat**

(2g sat fat), 204mg chol, 1038mg sodium, 24g carb, 0g fiber, 2g sugar, 70g protein

PIRI-PIRI CHICKEN

Serves 6

The name piri-piri in Swahili means chili-chili. Without question, it's definitely a spicy dish. Make sure your grill grates are sprayed with non-stick cooking spray beforehand, so the chicken skin doesn't stick to the grill and tear away. This chicken is both hot-hot and good-good!

Instructions

1. Rinse the chicken, butterfly*, and set aside. Melt the butter in a saucepan. Combine with the olive oil, lemon juice, hot sauce, paprika, ground coriander, garlic, scallions, parsley, ginger, bay leaves, and pepper in a blender and purée until smooth. Reserve half the marinade and refrigerate. Marinate the chicken with the remaining marinade and refrigerate for a minimum of 4 to 5 hours.

2. Place reserved, refrigerated marinade in a small saucepan and warm over a low heat. Heat the grill to 425°F (high setting). Place chicken breast side-up on the grill. Baste with the marinade and close grill lid for 15 minutes. Reduce heat to low and cook for another 45 minutes with the grill lid closed, or until internal temperature reaches 165°F. Baste the chicken generously, then carefully flip the chicken over to brown the skin for 5 to 10 minutes. Remove chicken from grill, wrap in foil, and allow to rest for 5 minutes. Carve chicken and place in a serving dish. Drizzle with warm leftover marinade. Serve with rice and pass around the remaining warm marinade as a sauce.

Grill

You'll Need

- 1 whole chicken, 3½ lb.
- 2 tablespoons salted butter
- ¼ cup extra-virgin olive oil
- ½ cup fresh lemon juice
- 2 tablespoons Tabasco (or habanero sauce if you like it hot!)
- 1 tablespoon paprika
- 1 teaspoon ground coriander
- 3 garlic cloves, chopped
- 3 scallions, chopped
- 3 tablespoons fresh parsley, chopped
- 1½ teaspoons chopped fresh ginger root
- 2 bay leaves, crumbled
- ½ teaspoon black pepper

*How to Butterfly a Chicken

You'll need a cutting board, a good sharp knife, and poultry shears. Using the poultry shears, cut along both sides of the backbone, removing it completely. Turn the chicken over and lay it out; press into the middle to break the wishbone. Flip the chicken over again and cut away the membrane holding the meat to the keel bone. Slide your thumbs up both sides of the keel bone to loosen the meat from it. Use your poultry shears to cut the end of the keel bone from the chicken and remove it. It's easier than it sounds.

MAKE IT LIGHTER

**472 calories
25g fat**

(3g sat fat), 173mg chol, 195mg sodium, 3g carb, 0g fiber, 0g sugar, 56g protein

**Before
712 calories
40g fat**

(8g sat fat), 268mg chol, 631mg sodium, 4g carb, 0g fiber, 0g sugar, 84g protein

ABOVE: At Fox and Friends with Clayton and my family
RIGHT: Clayton with his wife Natali

CLAYTON'S GLUTEN-FREE FRIED CHICKEN

Serves 4

I first met Clayton at *Fox and Friends Weekend* in NYC. They have such a great team there—both in front of the camera and behind. Clayton is an amazing guy and we certainly share a love of delicious food. I've admired his healthy eating choices and I'm grateful he and his wife Natali shared this gluten-free fried chicken recipe with us. This gives Clayton and me (and now you) a gluten-free alternative for feeding our families.

Instructions

Marinade: Mix yogurt, milk, vinegar, hot sauce, salt, and pepper. Refrigerate and soak chicken in the mixture for at least 2 hours or overnight.

1. Fill Butterball® or Masterbuilt fryer with oil. Heat to 375°F; this will take approximately 15 to 20 minutes.

2. Mix gluten-free flour, paprika, salt, and pepper in a paper sack. Take chicken out of marinade, pat dry, and place in paper sack. Shake to coat the chicken.

3. Place 3 to 5 pieces of chicken in the oil to fry at a time—enough to be in a single layer but not too crowded. Fry 10 to 14 minutes on each side. Internal temperature of the chicken should be at least 165°F when it is fully cooked.

4. Preheat oven to 200°F. Remove chicken from oil and drain on several layers of paper towels. Transfer to a baking sheet and put in the oven to keep warm while you fry the rest of the chicken.

LEFT:
Clayton gets two thumbs up from me!

Fryer

You'll need:

- 1¼ lbs. boneless chicken thighs and breasts
- 1 gallon canola oil
- 1 teaspoon pepper
- 2 cups gluten-free all-purpose flour, such as Trader Joe's Gluten-Free Flour
- 2 tablespoons paprika
- 1 teaspoon kosher salt
- 1 teaspoon pepper

Marinade:

- ½ cup whole milk plain yogurt
- 4 cups whole milk
- 1 tablespoon white vinegar
- ⅓ cup hot sauce
- ¼ cup kosher salt
- 1 teaspoon black pepper

ALL-TIME FAVORITE

Eating gluten-free can be a challenge. Removing gluten from the diet does not necessarily lower calories or fat. For a lower-calorie version of this recipe, slice a few pieces of the fried chicken and place atop cooked brown rice and steamed veggies.

**522 calories
29g fat**

(4g sat fat), 110mg chol, 718mg sodium, 31g carb, 2g fiber, 1g sugar, 32g protein

5
MAINS
POULTRY

I first met Rachael Ray at QVC. I was invited to appear on her show and we had a great time frying turkeys indoors. The segment was a hit and she invited me back and challenged me to develop a recipe for her "Buffalo Ranch-giving." The entire show was buffalo ranch themed. I worked with Team Masterbuilt to develop this recipe and Rachael loved it so much, we named it after her. I'm so grateful to have had the opportunity to work with Rachael and her team—they are dadgum good folks!

ABOVE: Alicia, Tonya, and me with Rachael after the show

HEALTHY ALTERNATIVE

TURKEY AND QUINOA SALAD

Enjoy this all-time favorite turkey sliced on a salad with cooked quinoa, celery, and cucumbers. Add some heirloom cherry tomatoes for color and flavor.

**149 calories
1g fat**

(0g sat fat), 20mg chol, 523mg sodium, 21g carb, 2g fiber, 1g sugar, 14g protein

Recipe based on ½ cup sliced turkey without skin, ½ cup cooked quinoa, 3 slices cucumber, ¼ cup chopped celery, 4 cherry tomatoes, 1 T. oil and vinegar dressing. (Serves 1)

BUFFALO RANCH TURKEY FOR RACHAEL

Serves 10

Instructions

1. Thaw turkey, if frozen. To properly thaw a frozen turkey in the refrigerator allow approximately 24 hours for every 4 pounds. Fill deep fryer with 2 gallons of oil and heat to 375°F. Remove giblets and neck. If present, remove and discard plastic leg holder and pop-up timer. Rinse turkey thoroughly with warm water or completely cover with warm water and soak for no more than 30 minutes to ensure cavity is free of ice.

2. Pat turkey completely dry on outside and inside of cavity with paper towels. Whisk together water and dry ranch seasoning. Using a marinade injection syringe, inject ½ cup (4 ounces) marinade in each breast. Inject ¼ cup (2 ounces) marinade into each leg and thigh. Optional: Sprinkle turkey generously with dry ranch seasoning, completely coating the outside of the turkey and inside of the cavity.

3. Place turkey, breast side up, in fryer basket. Slowly lower the basket into hot oil, being careful not to splatter hot oil. Fry turkey for 3 to 4 minutes per pound. Lift the basket from the hot oil slowly. Insert a meat thermometer in the meaty part of the breast; turkey is done when it reads 165°F. If the turkey is not done, lower it carefully back into the oil for an additional 5 minutes. Once the turkey reaches the desired temperature (minimum 165°F), remove from oil.

4. Allow the turkey to rest and drain in the fryer basket for about 10 minutes before removing for carving. Serve with buffalo sauce.

Buffalo Ranch Sauce: Mix ranch dressing with buffalo sauce. Season with dry Cajun seasoning to taste. Makes a great dipping sauce!

LEFT: Me, Rachael, and Tonya on-set at her show

Fryer

You'll Need

▶ 1 whole turkey, fresh or completely thawed (10 to 14 lbs.)

▶ 2 gallons cooking oil, preferably peanut oil

▶ 12 ounces water

▶ 9 tablespoons dry ranch seasoning (or 3, 1-ounce packets)

Buffalo Ranch Sauce

▶ ½ cup light ranch dressing

▶ 1 cup low-sodium buffalo sauce (any brand)

▶ Cajun seasoning

ALL-TIME FAVORITE

This turkey is amazing with its spicy ranch-dressing flavor. Slice and serve over quinoa and veggies for a refreshing and low-calorie salad.

**624 calories
44g fat**

(10g sat fat), 156mg chol, 1128mg sodium, 5g carb, 0g fiber, 0g sugar, 50g protein

5 MAINS POULTRY

BRINED CHICKEN WITH LEMON VINAIGRETTE

Serves 4

This chicken with lemon vinaigrette is so dadgum good, I would bet you won't have any leftovers. But, if you do, place the chicken in a shallow dish and drizzle with the vinaigrette and reheat. You can also cut up the chicken and serve over salad or pasta with the vinaigrette. There will be a significant difference in the grilling time for boneless versus bone-in chicken. Make sure you carefully monitor the internal temperature. The chicken is done when it reaches 165°F.

Instructions

1. In an extra-large bowl, combine chicken, water, ¼ cup of salt, and sugar. Cover and refrigerate overnight. Remove chicken, rinse to remove excess salt, and pat dry.

2. Preheat lightly greased grill to 400°F (medium-high setting). Grill chicken, with grill lid closed, turning occasionally, for 25 minutes or until internal temperature reaches 165°F and chicken is no longer pink inside. Drizzle with lemon vinaigrette; serve immediately. Garnish with lemon wedges.

Lemon Vinaigrette: In a blender or food processor, combine lemon juice, parsley, garlic, and pepper, and blend until smooth. With the machine running, gradually add oil through the feed tube. Set aside.

Option: You can also use bone-in chicken, which gets more tender results, but grill for 15 to 20 minutes longer or until internal temperature reaches 165°F.

Grill

You'll Need

- 3 lbs. assorted chicken pieces or whole chicken, cut up
- 2 quarts water
- ½ cup kosher salt
- 2 tablespoons granulated sugar

Lemon Vinaigrette:

- ¼ cup fresh lemon juice
- ¼ cup chopped fresh parsley
- 2 garlic cloves, peeled
- ¼ teaspoon freshly ground black pepper
- ⅓ cup olive oil

GOOD FOR YOU

Chicken and lemon are flavors that are often paired together, and for good reason. The lemon adds a tangy and citrus flavor to the chicken and may also act as a tenderizer.

**516 calories
26g fat**

(3g sat fat), 202mg chol, 918mg sodium, 1g carb, 0g fiber, 1g sugar, 68g protein

5 MAINS POULTRY

Fryer/Steamer

You'll Need

- 2 tablespoons extra-virgin olive oil
- 1 teaspoon minced garlic
- 1 large tomato, seeded and diced
- 2 scallions, including green tops, finely chopped
- 1 tablespoon fresh cilantro, chopped
- ¼ teaspoon crushed red pepper flakes
- ½ teaspoon sea salt
- 24 mussels, rinsed, scrubbed, and de-bearded
- ¼ cup white wine vinegar
- ¾ cup clam juice
- 1 lime, cut into wedges

GOOD FOR YOU

Cleaning mussels can get pretty labor intensive, so choose carefully. Look for a label on the bag indicating how and where the mussels were cultivated. Avoid wild mussels and look for grit-free "rope-cultured mussels."

**104 calories
6g fat**
(1g sat fat), 18mg chol, 580mg sodium, 4g carb, 1g fiber, 1g sugar, 10g protein

NEW ZEALAND MUSSELS

Serves 6

Before you get started, it's a good idea to make sure your mussels are fresh. Pick through the mussels and if you don't find any open ones, tap them sharply on the kitchen counter. If they don't close immediately, discard them. You can use the dull side of a paring knife to pull off the beards.

Instructions

1. Fill Butterball® or Masterbuilt fryer to the MAX fill line with water. Set to 375°F and bring to a boil. This will take approximately 15 to 20 minutes. Although cooking time on this recipe is short, water may need to be added if steamer is used for more than 60 minutes.

2. In a medium-size skillet, combine olive oil, garlic, tomato, scallions, cilantro, crushed red pepper flakes, and salt. Sauté for 3 minutes, or until vegetables are tender.

3. Using heavy-duty aluminum foil, make a foil packet to line the steamer basket. Place mussels in the foil-lined basket and pour tomato mixture over them. Pour vinegar and clam juice in packet next, then close packet and poke holes in top to let steam escape. Cover and steam for 8 minutes, or until mussels open. (Note: Do not lower basket into water when steaming.) Serve with lime wedges.

SALMON STEAKS WITH CITRUS SALSA

Serves 4   *Suggested wood chips for smoking: Alder*

Timing is critical when smoking salmon. Be careful not to overcook and dry out the salmon. The steaks should flake with a fork and be tender and juicy.

Instructions

1. In a small bowl, combine salt, pepper, lemon juice, lime juice (reserving 2 tablespoons for the salsa), basil, and brown sugar. Reserve 3 tablespoons of marinade for basting later. Place the salmon in a large bowl, cover with marinade, and refrigerate for a minimum of 30 to 45 minutes.

2. Load the wood tray with one small handful of wood chips and preheat the smoker to 225°F. Place salmon on middle smoker rack and smoke for 45 minutes to 1 hour, brushing occasionally with reserved marinade. Add more wood chips about every 30 minutes.

3. Serve topped with Citrus Salsa.

Citrus Salsa: In a medium bowl, combine papaya, pineapple, green onion, mango, cilantro, lime juice, salt, and sugar, mixing well.

Smoker

You'll Need

- ½ teaspoon sea salt
- 1 teaspoon black pepper
- ½ lemon, juiced
- 2 limes, juiced
- 1 tablespoon chopped fresh basil
- 1 tablespoon light brown sugar
- 4 salmon steaks, boned

Citrus Salsa:

- 3 cups diced, peeled papaya
- 2 cups diced fresh pineapple
- ½ cup chopped green onion
- 1 cup chopped ripe mango
- 2 tablespoons chopped cilantro
- 2 tablespoons lime juice
- ½ teaspoon salt
- 1 tablespoon sugar

5 MAINS FISH & SEAFOOD

You'll Need

- 1 gallon cooking oil
- $\frac{2}{3}$ cup dried bread crumbs
- 2 large eggs, beaten
- 1 tablespoon Dijon mustard
- 1 green onion, finely chopped
- $\frac{1}{2}$ teaspoon Worcestershire sauce
- $\frac{1}{4}$ teaspoon Butterball Cajun Seasoning
- 1 lb. fresh lump crab meat, cleaned and drained well

Sauce:

- 1 tablespoon light mayonnaise
- 2 tablespoons plain Greek yogurt
- 1 tablespoon mustard
- $\frac{1}{4}$ teaspoon paprika
- $\frac{1}{4}$ teaspoon hot sauce

CRAB CAKES

Serves 6

When it comes to crab meat, you definitely get what you pay for. If you want to impress your guests, go ahead and splurge on premium jumbo crab meat. If you want crab cakes without the extra cost, use a less expensive claw meat. One tip to get the best of both worlds is to mix the two. Either way, make sure the meat is fresh and moist, not mushy.

Instructions

1. Fill Butterball® or Masterbuilt fryer with oil. Heat to 375°F; this will take approximately 15 to 20 minutes.

2. Combine $\frac{1}{3}$ cup bread crumbs, eggs, mustard, green onion, Worcestershire sauce, and Butterball Cajun Seasoning in large bowl and mix well. Add the crab meat and mix well. With wet hands, form mixture into 6 cakes. Set aside.

3. Place the remaining $\frac{1}{3}$ cup bread crumbs into a shallow bowl. Dredge the crab cakes in crumbs and refrigerate, uncovered, for 1 hour.

4. Fry the crab cakes, turning once, about $1\frac{1}{2}$ minutes or until golden brown. Remove from oil and transfer to paper towels to drain.

Sauce: Mix mayonnaise, yogurt, mustard, paprika, and hot sauce in a small bowl and serve over crab cakes or as a spicy dipping sauce.

MAKE IT LIGHTER

262 calories
16g fat

(3g sat fat), 116mg chol, 419mg sodium, 10g carb, 1g fiber, 1g sugar, 18g protein

Before
383 calories
27g fat

(5g sat fat), 121mg chol, 546mg sodium, 14g carb, 1g fiber, 1g sugar, 18g protein

SHRIMP BOIL

Serves 6

When buying shrimp, I recommend easy-peel or already peeled with just the tail on so they are easy to serve and eat—especially for the kids. Remember, if they do not have the shell, they will cook faster, so cut the time down a bit.

Instructions

1. Fill Butterball® or Masterbuilt fryer to the MAX fill line with water. Set heat to boiling at 375°F and bring to a boil. This will take approximately 20 to 25 minutes.

2. Place liquid shrimp boil, Butterball Cajun Seasoning, and lemon juice into boiling water.

3. Add shrimp into the basket and lower basket into the boiling water. Cook for 8 to 10 minutes or until shrimp turns pink. Drain and serve with Cocktail Sauce.

Cocktail Sauce: In a small bowl, combine the ketchup, onion, horseradish, lemon juice, and tarragon. Serve with your favorite seafood. Serve as a dipping sauce. Makes 1 cup.

Fryer/Boiler

You'll Need

- 1 teaspoon liquid shrimp boil
- 1 teaspoon Butterball Cajun Seasoning
- ½ cup freshly squeezed lemon juice
- 2 to 5 lbs. raw medium shrimp

Cocktail Sauce:

- 1 cup low-sodium ketchup
- 3 tablespoons grated onion
- 3 tablespoons horseradish
- 2 tablespoons fresh lemon juice
- 2 tablespoons chopped fresh tarragon

MAKE IT LIGHTER

218 calories
3g fat

(1g sat fat), 255mg chol, 360mg sodium, 13g carb, 0g fiber, 7g sugar, 34g protein

Before
345 calories
5g fat

(1g sat fat), 255mg chol, 2291mg sodium, 22g carb, 1g fiber, 16g sugar, 53g protein

LOW COUNTRY BOIL

Serves 6

Nothing is better or easier for large and small crowds than our Low Country Boil. For a splash-free cooking experience, I recommend you hook the basket as you add each ingredient. If you like, you can substitute some of the shrimp with crawfish. Complete the experience and have a little fun by dumping the boil out on newspaper for a true "grab 'n' growl" — no forks required.

Instructions

1. Fill Butterball® or Masterbuilt fryer to the MAX fill line with water and Cajun seasoning. (NOTE: If using a seasoning bag, place bag in basket.) Set heat to 375°F and bring to a boil. This will take approximately 20 to 25 minutes.

2. Add whole potatoes to basket and lower carefully into boiling water; boil for 12 minutes.

3. Add corn to the potatoes, and boil an additional 9 minutes.

4. Add sausage to the potatoes and corn, continuing to boil for 9 more minutes.

5. Finally, add the shrimp. Boil for an additional 3 to 5 minutes until shrimp are pink. Total cooking time for the boil is 33 to 35 minutes. Lift the basket from the hot water slowly, hooking onto the side using drain clips. Allow Low Country Boil to drain, and serve hot.

LEFT: Another dadgum good low country boil at the McLemore House

Fryer/Boiler

You'll Need

- 1 tablespoon Butterball Cajun Seasoning (or your favorite seafood boil seasoning or bag)

- 2 lbs. whole new potatoes

- 8 to 12 pieces short-ear corn

- 2 lbs. pre-cooked smoked sausage, cut into ½- to 1-inch slices

- 2 lbs. raw shrimp, preferably split and deveined

ALL-TIME FAVORITE

This classic combination of potatoes, corn, sausage, and shrimp is a treat that can't be beat. You can use turkey sausage to cut the calories and still maintain the fresh mixture of flavors.

**754 calories
45g fat**

(14g sat fat), 255mg chol, 580mg sodium, 39g carb, 5g fiber, 4g sugar, 49g protein

5 MAINS FISH & SEAFOOD

FRIED FISH TACOS

Serves 6

My brother Don and I enjoy fishing with family and friends. While doing a fishing show with outdoorsman Dean Durham, we loaded up on large-mouth bass one day. Our thanks to Dean for a great start to our fish taco recipe that day!

Instructions

1. Fill Butterball® or Masterbuilt fryer with oil. Heat to 350°F; this will take approximately 15 to 20 minutes.

2. For the batter, combine 1 cup flour, salt, oregano, dry mustard, garlic salt, and pepper in a large bowl. Using a whisk, stir sparkling water into the flour mixture until well-blended. Set aside.

3. Rinse fish and pat dry with paper towels. Cut fillets into 12 (1x5-inch) pieces.

4. Place ½ cup flour in shallow bowl. Dredge fish in the flour. Dip fish into batter, taking care to coat all sides. Place about 3 pieces of fish in a single layer in hot oil. Cook in batches of three, about 2 minutes per side or until batter is crispy and golden brown.

5. Warm tortillas according to package directions. To assemble, layer a fish fillet, white sauce, salsa, avocado, and cabbage on each tortilla. Top with a squeeze of lime. Fold tortilla around ingredients to serve.

Salsa: In a medium bowl, combine tomatoes, onion, jalapeños, cilantro, salt, and lime juice. Refrigerate until ready to serve.

White Sauce: In a small bowl, mix mayonnaise, yogurt, cilantro, and lime juice until blended. Refrigerate until ready to serve.

ABOVE: Don and me with outdoorsman Dean Durham

ALL-TIME FAVORITE

For a healthier version of this recipe, grill the fish instead of frying. You'll still enjoy the great flavor combination.

532 calories
21g fat

(3g sat fat), 48mg chol, 428mg sodium, 57g carb, 9g fiber, 6g sugar, 31g protein

Fryer

You'll Need

- 1 gallon cooking oil
- 1½ cups unbleached all-purpose flour, divided
- ½ teaspoon salt
- ½ teaspoon dried oregano
- ½ teaspoon dry mustard
- ¼ teaspoon garlic salt
- ¼ teaspoon black pepper
- 1 cup sparkling water
- 1½ lbs. cod or bass
- 12 fresh stone-ground corn or flour tortillas
- 1 ripe avocado, peeled, pitted, and cut into slices
- 3 cups finely shredded cabbage
- 3 limes, cut into wedges

Salsa:

- 3 cups diced tomatoes
- ½ cup diced white onion
- 2 medium jalapeños, seeded and minced
- ½ cup fresh cilantro, chopped
- ½ teaspoon salt
- 1 tablespoon fresh lime juice

White Sauce:

- 2 tablespoons light mayonnaise
- ½ cup plain low-fat Greek yogurt
- ⅓ cup fresh cilantro, chopped
- 2 tablespoons lime juice

Needless to say, this recipe is an indulgence. My dad has been the most influential person in my life when it comes to hard work, doing the right thing no matter what and frying fish. Our family business has allowed us to work together, play together, and cook together and this recipe will always be one of my favorites. When I indulge, it better be worth it—and believe me, this recipe is worth it! In the South, a "fish fry" is about much more than the food. It's about sharing stories and spending time with the ones you love. Take a moment to indulge and enjoy!

BELOW: "The fish was THIS big!"

HEALTHY ALTERNATIVE

VEGGIE AND FISH SPINACH WRAP

Enjoy the fried fish without all of the calories by making a wrap filled with fish and healthy veggies.

**542 calories
24g fat**

(5g sat fat), 68mg chol, 801mg sodium, 54g carb, 5g fiber, 7g sugar, 29g protein

Recipe based on: 1 small fried fish fillet, sliced; ½ cup shredded coleslaw mixture; 1 T. light coleslaw dressing; 1 spinach tortilla wrap; 2 pineapple wedges. Mix coleslaw with dressing. Add fish and wrap in tortilla. Serve with pineapple wedges. (Serves 1)

PAWPAW'S OLD FASHIONED SOUTHERN FRIED FISH & HUSH PUPPIES

Serves 8

Instructions

1. Fill Butterball® or Masterbuilt fryer with oil. Heat to 375°F; this will take approximately 15 to 20 minutes.

2. Thaw fish (if frozen). Clean the fish and season with salt. Coat fish with cornmeal, shaking off any excess coating. Place fish into hot oil and cook for 3½ minutes per side. Fish should be golden brown on both sides, crusty on the outside and moist and flaky on the inside. Allow the fish to drain in fryer basket before removing.

Hush Puppies:

1. Combine cornmeal, flour, baking soda, egg, and onion in medium bowl. Stirring, add buttermilk until the consistency is thick enough to form golf ball-sized hush puppies. Add optional ingredients, if desired.

2. Drop the batter, 1 tablespoon at a time, into the oil. Dip the spoon in a glass of water to clean it after each hush puppy is dropped into the oil. Fry hush puppies for 4 to 6 minutes, until golden brown, turning the hush puppies during the cooking process to cook evenly. Allow the hush puppies to drain in fryer basket before removing.

Fryer

You'll Need

▶ 1 gallon cooking oil

▶ 4 lbs. fresh or frozen catfish fillets or whiting fish (about 24 fillets)

▶ 2 teaspoons salt

▶ 3 cups cornmeal

Hush Puppies:

▶ 2 cups yellow cornmeal

▶ ½ cup self-rising flour

▶ Pinch of baking soda

▶ 1 large egg, lightly beaten

▶ ¼ cup chopped yellow onion

▶ 1½ cups buttermilk

▶ ¼ cup chopped jalapeño, ½ cup grated Cheddar cheese, or ½ cup corn (optional)

LEFT: Helping the Ole' man fry some fish

ALL-TIME FAVORITE

Portion control is the answer here. Just don't eat too much of a good thing!

(fish and hush puppies)
1244 calories
64g fat
(13g sat fat), 234mg chol, 878mg sodium, 88g carb, 4g fiber, 4g sugar, 79g protein

BROOKE'S BOILED LOBSTER

Serves 2

Most dads who spoil their kids do so with name brand clothes and expensive cars—for my kids, it's with food! Steak and lobster to be specific. It's interesting that those foods are my daughter Brooke's favorites because that's exactly what I cooked for their mom on our first date. I guess you could say it's in their blood.

Instructions

1. Fill Butterball® or Masterbuilt fryer with water to the MAX line. Set heat to 375°F and bring to a boil. This will take approximately 20 to 25 minutes.

2. Place lobster in basket and lower into water. Cover and boil for 15 minutes or until internal temperature reaches 140°F and lobster is bright red.

Sauce: Combine sauce ingredients in a small saucepan over medium heat. Cook 3 to 4 minutes or until butter is melted. Makes ¾ cup sauce.

Fryer/Boiler

You'll Need

- 2 (1½ lb.) live lobsters

Sauce:

- ¼ cup butter
- 1 teaspoon grated lemon rind
- 1 tablespoon lemon juice
- 1 teaspoon grated orange rind
- 1 tablespoon orange juice
- 2 tablespoons chopped fresh chives
- 1 tablespoon chopped fresh parsley
- ¼ teaspoon cayenne pepper
- ¼ teaspoon salt

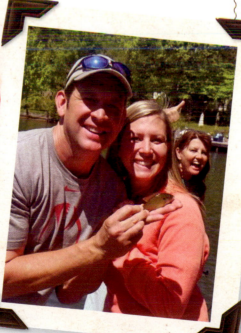

ABOVE: I love my "Brookie Cookie"!
RIGHT: Brooke's giant catch (and Tonya's photobombing!)

GOOD FOR YOU

Whether you pull a lobster straight out of the tank in the store or from the sea, its tail should be flopping. If it is limp, that is a sign of a soon-to-be-dead lobster.

340 calories
24g fat

(15g sat fat), 204mg chol, 593mg sodium, 1g carb, 1g fiber, 0g sugar, 28g protein

SHIRLEY'S SALMON PATTIES

Serves 6

My mother-in-law Shirley is the greatest mother-in-law a guy could have. She's had fun with what she calls the "celebrity lifestyle" from having a recipe in my last book. When we told her we planned to include her recipe in this new book, she was thrilled to continue with her "stardom!" Of course, we're kidding here, but she sure is a star in our hearts.

Instructions

1. Fill Butterball® or Masterbuilt fryer with oil. Heat to 350°F; this will take approximately 15 to 20 minutes.

2. Remove skin from salmon and chop in a food processor or with a knife; do not over process. In a large bowl, combine salmon, ½ cup crackers, onion, eggs, Cajun seasoning, cracked peppercorns, and Greek dressing.

3. Using a ⅓ cup measure for each patty, shape mixture into 6 patties. Roll each in remaining crushed crackers.

4. Place in fryer, turning once, and fry for 2½ to 3 minutes or until patties are golden brown and float to the top. Use a metal slotted spoon to transfer to paper towels to drain. Serve with your favorite sauce.

Fryer

You'll Need

- ▶ 1 gallon cooking oil
- ▶ 2 lbs. fresh salmon
- ▶ 1 sleeve saltine crackers, crushed, divided
- ▶ ½ cup chopped yellow onion
- ▶ 2 eggs, well beaten
- ▶ ½ teaspoon Cajun seasoning
- ▶ ⅛ teaspoon cracked black peppercorns
- ▶ ¼ cup Ken's Steakhouse Greek Dressing

ABOVE: Shirley and her husband Jon help at a Masterbuilt event.

ALL-TIME FAVORITE

Salmon patties are an all-time favorite dish. Fried foods are high in fat and calories, but you can minimize the fat absorbed by only adding the patties when the grease is hot and keeping the temperature hot by not adding too many patties at one time.

**584 calories
41g fat**

(8g sat fat), 156mg chol, 631mg sodium, 17g carb, 1g fiber, 1g sugar, 36g protein

5 MAINS FISH & SEAFOOD

STEAMED SALMON WITH CREOLE SAUCE

Serves 6

If you looked over the index of recipes in all of my cookbooks, you would swear my hometown was New Orleans! I absolutely love creole and Cajun flavors. I'm from Georgia, but I must have a little Cajun blood in me somewhere! Those flavors add value to so many recipes and they pair especially well with this steamed salmon.

Instructions

1. Fill Butterball® or Masterbuilt fryer to the MAX fill line with water. Set to 375°F and bring to a boil. This will take approximately 15 to 20 minutes. Although cooking time on this recipe is short, water may need to be added if steamer is used for more than 60 minutes.

2. Rub olive oil on salmon steaks and sprinkle them with Butterball® Cajun Seasoning. Place salmon steaks in the basket and, using the drain clip, hook basket onto inner pot. (Note: Do not lower basket into water when steaming.) Cover and steam for 12 to 15 minutes.

3. Remove salmon from steamer. Plate salmon steaks and sprinkle with parsley. Top with Creole Sauce and serve with lemon wedges.

Creole Sauce:

1. In a large skillet, heat butter over medium-high heat until melted. Add tomatoes, onion, green pepper, celery, and garlic, then sauté for 8 minutes, or until vegetables are tender. Add bouillon cube, pepper, oregano, basil, hot sauce, and bay leaves and bring to a boil.

2. Reduce heat and simmer, covered, for 20 minutes, stirring occasionally. Remove bay leaves just before serving. Makes 2 cups.

Fryer/Steamer

You'll Need

- 6, 6-ounce salmon steaks
- 1 tablespoon extra-virgin olive oil
- ½ teaspoon Butterball Cajun Seasoning
- 2 tablespoons chopped fresh parsley
- Lemon wedges

Creole Sauce:

- 2 tablespoons butter
- 1 can (15-ounces) diced tomatoes with roasted garlic and onion, undrained
- ⅔ cup chopped yellow onion
- ⅔ cup chopped green bell pepper
- ⅔ cup chopped celery
- 2 teaspoons minced garlic
- 1 reduced-sodium chicken-flavored bouillon cube
- ½ teaspoon coarsely ground black pepper
- ½ teaspoon oregano
- ½ teaspoon basil
- ¼ teaspoon hot sauce
- 2 bay leaves

MAKE IT LIGHTER

439 calories
29g fat
(8g sat fat), 104mg chol, 372mg sodium, 6g carb, 2g fiber, 3g sugar, 36g protein

Before
660 calories
43g fat
(17g sat fat), 109mg chol, 1335mg sodium, 9g carb, 0g fiber, 4g sugar, 57g protein

ABOVE: Hunting with J-Mac, Glenn, and Jeff

GLENN'S SMOKED BBQ SHRIMP

Serves 6   *Suggested wood chips for smoking: Alder*

Glenn Scarborough is our CFO at Masterbuilt. Glenn loves to eat most anything and he is always quick to respond when we need taste-testers in MeMaw's Kitchen. He doesn't mind coming back for seconds either! One day when Glenn retires, we will most likely still see him around Masterbuilt, since he's a part of our family and one of the chief taste-testers!

Instructions

1. Load the wood tray with a small handful of wood chips and preheat the smoker to 225°F.

2. In a medium-size bowl, mix together melted butter, dressing, pepper, garlic powder, Worcestershire sauce, apple juice, and Butterball® Cajun Seasoning. Place washed and drained shrimp with shells-on in a large disposable aluminum pan and cover with the liquid mixture.

3. Place pan of shrimp on middle rack of smoker and cook, uncovered for 1½ hours or until internal temperature reaches 145°F. Stir the shrimp halfway through the smoking process. Serve with French bread for dipping in the shrimp sauce, if desired.

ABOVE: Glenn and his wife Nancy

Smoker

You'll Need

- ½ cup (1 stick) butter, melted
- 12 ounces reduced-fat Italian dressing
- 1 tablespoon black pepper
- 2 teaspoons garlic powder
- ¼ cup Worcestershire sauce
- ¼ cup apple juice
- ¼ teaspoon Butterball Cajun Seasoning
- 5 lbs. raw medium shrimp (shell-on)

MAKE IT LIGHTER

**472 calories
16g fat**

(6g sat fat), 532mg chol, 596mg sodium, 5g carb, 0g fiber, 2g sugar, 77g protein

**Before
749 calories
45g fat**

(17g sat fat), 635mg chol, 1448mg sodium, 9g carb, 0g fiber, 4g sugar, 77g protein

You'll Need

- ▶ 6 1-inch thick tuna steaks
- ▶ 2 cups water
- ▶ ¼ cup packed brown sugar
- ▶ 1 teaspoon kosher salt
- ▶ ½ teaspoon cayenne pepper
- ▶ 2 tablespoons olive oil, divided
- ▶ Juice of 2 limes
- ▶ ½ teaspoon Jane's Krazy Mixed-Up Salt
- ▶ ¾ teaspoon ground ginger

GRILLED TUNA STEAKS

Serves 6

When you cook the marinade for these grilled tuna steaks, be sure to let it cool completely before pouring over the steaks. Otherwise, the hot marinade could cook the steaks in the fridge. The thickness of the steaks will determine the grilling time. Be sure to watch them carefully because tuna cooks quickly on the grill. You don't want to dry the steaks out. I prefer mine cooked to medium, but you can leave them rare and just sear on the outside if you prefer them that way.

Instructions

1. Place steaks in a disposable aluminum foil pan. In a medium saucepan, combine water, brown sugar, kosher salt, and cayenne pepper. Cook on low heat until brown sugar and salt are dissolved. Let cool so that the marinade does not "cook" the steaks. Pour cooled marinade over steaks. Cover and place in refrigerator and marinate for 3 hours, turning once.

2. Preheat lightly greased grill to 450°F (high setting). Remove steaks from marinade; discard marinade. Place steaks on a baking sheet and baste each steak with 1 teaspoon olive oil. Pour lime juice over steaks. In a small bowl, combine Krazy salt and ground ginger. Gently press into steaks.

3. Grill steaks for 2 minutes per side, with grill lid closed, or until internal temperature reaches 145°F. Serve immediately.

MAKE IT LIGHTER

251 calories
5g fat

(0g sat fat), 53mg chol, 351mg sodium, 6g carb, 0g fiber, 5g sugar, 44g protein

Before
272 calories
5g fat

(0g sat fat), 53mg chol, 862mg sodium, 12g carb, 0g fiber, 11g sugar, 44g protein

FISH JAMBALAYA

Serves 6 *Suggested wood chips for smoking: Alder*

Jambalaya is another one of those dishes you can customize by changing out the flavors with your choice of fish or other ingredients. Don't feel tied to the recipe each time you make it. Also, you can adjust the spices depending on your heat tolerance.

Instructions

1. Load the wood tray with one small handful of wood chips and preheat the smoker to 225°F. Place the fish on the top rack of the smoker and cook for 45 minutes, or until internal temperature reaches 145°F.

2. While fish is in the smoker, lightly brown the onions in oil in a large frying pan. Add the potatoes and fry until golden brown. Stir in the jalapeños, ginger, tomatoes, and vegetable stock. Cook over a low heat for 5 minutes.

3. Remove smoked fish from smoker and flake, then add to frying pan. Add rice and yellow raisins, spoon mixture to serving plates and season with lemon juice, and salt and pepper to taste.

Smoker

You'll Need

- 4 fish fillets, boned and skinned (preferably Amberjack, or favorite fish)
- 2 medium yellow onions, finely sliced
- 2 tablespoons extra-virgin olive oil
- 3 large red potatoes (2 cups), peeled and cubed
- 2 jalapeños, seeded and finely chopped
- 1 teaspoon fresh ginger, finely chopped
- 1 can (14-ounces) no-salt diced tomatoes
- ¾ cup low-sodium vegetable stock
- 2 cups cooked brown rice
- ¼ cup yellow raisins
- 3 tablespoons freshly squeezed lemon juice
- Salt and black pepper to taste

MAKE IT LIGHTER

344 calories
13g fat

(3g sat fat), 50mg chol, 91mg sodium, 35g carb, 4g fiber, 8g sugar, 20g protein

Before
364 calories
17g fat

(5g sat fat), 60mg chol, 358mg sodium, 32g carb, 3g fiber, 7g sugar, 20g protein

Grill

You'll Need

- ▸ 2 tablespoon vegetable oil
- ▸ 1 tablespoon horseradish
- ▸ 2 tablespoon low-sodium soy sauce
- ▸ 1 clove garlic, minced
- ▸ 6, 6-ounce salmon fillets, (1-inch thick, skin-on)
- ▸ Salt and pepper to taste

Sauce:

- ▸ ¾ cup plain Greek yogurt
- ▸ ¼ cup low-fat mayonnaise
- ▸ 2 tablespoons horseradish
- ▸ 2 tablespoons chopped fresh basil
- ▸ 1 tablespoon fresh lemon juice
- ▸ 1 teaspoon low-sodium soy sauce

MAKE IT LIGHTER

This unique and delicious salmon recipe is loaded with heart-healthy omega-3 fats.

425 calories
28g fat
(5g sat fat), 94mg chol, 397mg sodium, 3g carb, 0g fiber, 3g sugar, 39g protein

Before
591 calories
48g fat
(12g sat fat), 97mg chol, 599mg sodium, 3g carb, 0g fiber, 3g sugar, 36g protein

GRILLED SALMON

Serves 6

My best memories of salmon fishing are from a trip to Puget Sound in Washington state. Salmon is now an important part of my diet. Looks like I need to head back to Puget Sound soon! All I need is an excuse to travel and fishing with my family is on the agenda.

Instructions

1. Spray grill rack generously with nonstick spray. Preheat grill to 350°F (medium setting).

2. Combine oil, horseradish, soy sauce, and garlic. Stir well. After sprinkling salmon with salt and pepper to taste, baste both sides of the salmon with this mixture.

3. Cook the fillets for approximately 4 minutes on each side, until flaky and opaque. Enjoy with sauce!

Sauce: Stir together yogurt, mayonnaise, horseradish, basil, lemon juice, and soy sauce. Add salt and pepper to taste. Cover and chill until serving.

STEAMED CRAB LEGS

Serves 4

I can't make this recipe without thinking of my son J-Mac. We were at QVC one day and had just completed an airing for the Butterball Indoor Electric Turkey Fryer. This fryer also steams and boils, so there were 10 lbs. of crab legs on-set. We walked off set for a while and when we returned J-Mac was sitting beside the leftover shells of 10 lbs. of crab legs! He ate every single one and he was miserable! I don't recommend eating 10 lbs. of these in one sitting, but enjoy in moderation for sure.

Fryer/Steamer

You'll Need

▸ 1½ lbs. king crab legs, split and thawed

▸ 1 teaspoon salt

▸ 2 teaspoons crab boil

▸ Lemon wedges, melted butter (optional)

Instructions

1. Fill Butterball® or Masterbuilt Fryer to the MAX fill line with water. Set to 375°F and bring to a boil. Add salt and crab boil. This will take approximately 15 to 20 minutes. Although cooking time on this recipe is short, water may need to be added if steamer is used for more than 60 minutes.

2. Add the crab legs to basket. Using the drain clip, hook basket onto the inner pot. Do not lower basket into water when steaming. As the water starts to boil again, begin timing. Steam the crab legs for 15 to 20 minutes, until you begin to smell their aroma. Make sure not to overcook the legs. Remove from the heat and serve hot with melted butter and lemon wedges or other favorite sauce.

ABOVE: Yes, you can steam crab legs in a turkey fryer!

GOOD FOR YOU

Steamed crab legs are very low in saturated fat and a good source of vitamin C, folate, and magnesium. So enjoy in good health!

141 calories
1g fat

(0g sat fat), 72mg chol, 385mg sodium, 0g carb, 0g fiber, 0g sugar, 31g protein

Smoker

You'll Need

- 1 tablespoon paprika
- 1 teaspoon ground cumin
- 1 teaspoon black pepper
- ¼ teaspoon salt
- 1 teaspoon onion powder
- ¼ teaspoon cayenne pepper
- 7 catfish fillets (2½ lbs.)

Marinade Sauce:

- ½ cup low-sodium chicken stock
- ½ cup orange juice
- 2 tablespoons lime juice
- 2 tablespoons vegetable oil

ABOVE: I had to come home and see the fish J-Mac caught on his own!

GOOD FOR YOU

289 calories
20g fat
(4g sat fat), 75mg chol, 90mg sodium, 1g carb, 0g fiber, 1g sugar, 25g protein

SPICY CUBAN SMOKED CATFISH

Serves 7   *Suggested wood chips for smoking: Alder*

Anytime I make a fish recipe, I'm reminded of all the great times spent fishing with my family. One particular time, my son J-Mac decided he didn't need any help from the family and went fishing all on his own. We live on a lake, and he went to the garage one day and grabbed a fishing pole with a bass lure already on it. He walked down to the lake, cast the line, caught a catfish, and dragged it all the way back to the house! I should mention that he was only 4 years old at the time! My wife called and said she didn't know whether to be mad, scared, or proud! She took a photo and a scary moment turned into yet another memory for our family.

Instructions

1. In a small bowl, combine the paprika, cumin, pepper, salt, onion powder, and cayenne pepper to make a rub. Reserve 1 tablespoon for Marinade Sauce.

2. Coat catfish fillets with rub. Lay fillets flat in a large pan; cover with Marinade Sauce, reserving ¼ cup of sauce for basting later. Refrigerate fillets for at least 3 hours.

3. Load the wood tray with one small handful of wood chips and preheat the smoker to 180°F.

4. Remove fish from sauce, and smoke the catfish on the top rack for 1 to 1½ hours. Baste with reserved Marinade Sauce every 20 minutes. The catfish is done when it is flaky and white on the inside.

Marinade Sauce: In a medium bowl, whisk the chicken stock, orange juice, lime juice, oil, and reserved rub.

RAMON'S STEAMED FISH WRAPPED IN BANANA LEAVES

Serves 4

Ramon is a valuable part of Team Masterbuilt. He works in our warehouse, and I found out one day during a company fish-fry that he loves to cook. Although he's not a culinary school graduate, he cooked in several restaurants and brought some mean cookin' skills to Masterbuilt. Thanks to Ramon for sharing this recipe and his expertise!

Instructions

1. Fill Butterball® or Masterbuilt Fryer to the MAX fill line with water. Set to 375°F and bring to a boil. This will take approximately 15 to 20 minutes. Although cooking time on this recipe is short, water may need to be added if steamer is used for more than 60 minutes.

2. In a small mixing bowl, mix the oil, lemon juice, and garlic. Add salt and pepper. Mix well. Brush both sides of the fish with the lemon mixture.

3. Lay 4 lemon slices and 2 onion slices on top of each fish. Place two of the banana leaves on top of one another, forming a cross. Place the fish in the center of the leaves. Wrap the fish in the leaves, securing the fish with toothpicks. Place the fish pouches in the basket. Do not lower basket into water when steaming. Steam for 4 to 6 minutes. Serve with sautéed vegetables.

Fryer/Steamer

You'll Need

- ½ cup olive oil
- ¼ cup fresh lemon juice
- 1 tablespoon chopped fresh garlic
- ¼ teaspoon sea salt
- ½ teaspoon freshly ground black pepper
- 4, 6- to 8-ounce bass or cod fillets
- 16 thin slices of fresh lemon
- 8 large banana leaves, soaked in water
- 8 onion slices
- 12 toothpicks, (soaked in water) or string

RIGHT:
Ramon fried up some fish for the warehouse crew.

5
MAINS
FISH & SEAFOOD

GOOD FOR YOU

389 calories
19g fat

(3g sat fat), 99mg chol, 317mg sodium, 12g carb, 3g fiber, 5g sugar, 43g protein

You'll Need:

- 2 lbs. raw medium shrimp (shells on) (21 to 30 count)
- 1 medium or large lemon, cut into wedges

Seafood Spice Mix:

- 1 tablespoon chili powder
- 1 tablespoon paprika
- ¼ teaspoon cayenne pepper
- 1 bay leaf, finely ground
- ½ teaspoon dry mustard
- 1 teaspoon dried oregano
- ½ teaspoon salt
- ½ teaspoon black pepper
- 1 teaspoon granulated sugar
- ½ teaspoon coriander seed, ground

GOOD FOR YOU

**123 calories
2g fat**

(0g sat fat), 170mg chol, 819mg sodium, 2g carb, 0g fiber, 1g sugar, 23g protein

STEAMED SPICY SHRIMP

Serves 4

This recipe calls for serving with lemon wedges. To change the flavors up a bit, switch the lemons out with limes. Squeeze the limes over the shrimp before serving for a new twist of flavor.

Instructions

1. Fill Butterball® or Masterbuilt Fryer to the MAX fill line with water. Set to 375°F and bring to a boil. This will take approximately 15 to 20 minutes. Although cooking time on this recipe is short, water may need to be added if steamer is used for more than 60 minutes.

2. In a small bowl, mix all ingredients for the Seafood Spice Mix. Place shrimp in a large bowl and sprinkle with the spice mix. Place shrimp in basket. Using the drain clip, hook basket onto the inner pot. (Note: Do not lower basket into water when steaming.) Cover and steam shrimp for 6 to 8 minutes or until shrimp turns pink. Serve the shrimp with lemon wedges and a dish of the spices or your favorite cocktail sauce for dipping.

LEFT: Bailey and Alicia enjoying some fried shrimp before we swapped them out for steamed

DANNY'S FISH RUB AND FISH

Serves 6

Danny East has been with Masterbuilt for many years. To say he loves fishing is an understatement. In fact, Danny wears fishing shirts to Masterbuilt almost every single day. I suspect it's because on any given day, he's likely to go fishing right after work—or maybe even during his lunch break! If you're looking for a great fish rub there's no better expert than Danny.

Instructions

1. Spray grill rack generously with nonstick spray. Preheat grill to 350°F (medium setting).

2. Make rub by combining Old Bay Seasoning, garlic powder, onion, paprika, salt, cilantro, and olive oil. Rub generously on both sides of the fillets.

3. Lay lemon slice on each fillet and grill the fillets for approximately 4 minutes on each side, until flaky and opaque. Enjoy with favorite sauce.

Grill

You'll need:

- ▸ 6 fish fillets such as catfish or cod

- ▸ Lemon slices

Spice Rub:

- ▸ 2 teaspoons Old Bay Seasoning

- ▸ 2 teaspoons garlic powder

- ▸ 1 tablespoon minced onion

- ▸ 1 tablespoon paprika

- ▸ 1 teaspoon sea salt

- ▸ ¼ cup fresh cilantro leaves

- ▸ 2 tablespoons olive oil

RIGHT: Danny and his daughter Linzy at a Fishers of Men dinner

5 MAINS FISH & SEAFOOD

GOOD FOR YOU

Most rubs contain a great deal of sodium. So if you are trying to limit sodium, use them sparingly.

285 calories
18g fat
(4g sat fat), 80mg chol, 550mg sodium, 3g carb, 1g fiber, 1g sugar, 27g protein

6 DESSERTS

If you're one of those folks who could start a meal with dessert, it can be difficult to find healthy options to satisfy your sweet cravings. We've given you some dadgum good dessert choices using fresh fruits and low-fat ingredients, so you won't have to feel guilty about having your dessert and eating it, too!

TOP: Sharing a donut bar on a morning television show
ABOVE: These sundaes are crazy good!

GRILLED BANANA SUNDAES

Serves 4

When enjoying ice cream, our natural tendency is to add even more sugary toppings. I've found that to create more balance in my diet, it's better to add smarter toppings, like fruit. Grilling these bananas brings out the flavor and they are a nice pairing with frozen yogurt.

Instructions:

1. Preheat lightly greased grill to 350°F (medium setting).

2. Cut bananas in half lengthwise. Cut each piece in half crosswise. Place in a large shallow dish.

3. In a small bowl, stir together butter, cinnamon, and vanilla. Brush butter mixture on both sides of bananas.

4. Grill bananas for 2 minutes on each side or until heated through. Be sure to use a spatula to move the bananas around gently during the grilling process to prevent sticking. Scoop frozen yogurt into 4 serving dishes. Top evenly with bananas and add your favorite ice cream toppings.

Grill

You'll Need

- ▶ 4 large ripe firm bananas
- ▶ 2 tablespoons butter, melted
- ▶ ¼ teaspoon ground cinnamon
- ▶ ¼ teaspoon vanilla extract
- ▶ 1 pint frozen vanilla yogurt
- ▶ Toppings: (optional) sprinkles, toasted coconut, maraschino cherries, fresh berries, pecans

MAKE IT LIGHTER

The grilling process helps the cinnamon, butter, and vanilla caramelize onto the bananas, adding flavor that far surpasses a plain ol' banana sundae!

353 calories
15g fat

(7g sat fat), 28mg chol, 145mg sodium, 50g carb, 3g fiber, 22g sugar, 7g protein

Before
539 calories
33g fat

(16g sat fat), 53mg chol, 180mg sodium, 56g carb, 4g fiber, 23g sugar, 5g protein

6 DESSERTS

In over 20 years at QVC, by far, I've never met another host who loves food and cooking as much as David Venable. I'm grateful that David honored me with writing the foreword to this book, but I'm even more grateful that I get to cook alongside him at QVC.

TOP: Me and the family with David at QVC
CENTER: David honored me with a Golden Spatula Award!
BELOW: Enjoying some smoked salmon with David

DAVID'S LOW-FAT FROZEN PEANUT BUTTER PIE

Serves 8

David Venable is a true foodie and I've learned a lot while following his show. It's safe to say that I'm a big David Venable fan and proud to call him friend! You'll love his low-fat frozen peanut butter pie!

Instructions

1. Place the cream cheese and peanut butter into the bowl of a stand mixer, fitted with a paddle attachment, and beat until evenly combined. Add the confectioner's sugar and vanilla extract and mix until fully incorporated, stopping occasionally to scrape down the sides of bowl.

2. Reduce the mixer speed to low and add the 12-ounce container whipped topping in three stages, mixing well after each addition and stopping to scrape down the sides and bottom of the bowl. The mixture should be light and fluffy when it's ready. Evenly spoon the peanut butter mixture into the chocolate cookie pie crust. Freeze for two hours.

3. Remove the pie from the freezer and spread the 4-ounce container of whipped topping evenly on top of the peanut butter mixture. Place the pie back in the freezer and freeze for 2 hours, or overnight. Before cutting the pie, drizzle on some chocolate sauce. Sprinkle with chopped chocolate peanut butter cups and, if desired, peanuts on top.

You'll Need

Peanut Butter Filling:

- 4 ounces fat-free cream cheese, softened
- ¾ cup reduced-fat creamy peanut butter
- 1 cup confectioner's sugar
- 1 teaspoon vanilla extract
- 1 container (12-ounces) fat-free whipped topping
- 1 (9-inch) ready-to-use chocolate cookie pie crust

Topping:

- 1 container (4-ounces) fat-free whipped topping
- Purchased chocolate sauce
- 6 chocolate peanut butter cups, chopped

ALL-TIME FAVORITE

This dessert is sure to become your favorite pie! It is low in fat and has protein because of the peanut butter. So enjoy!

**494 calories
16g fat**

(3g sat fat), 1mg chol, 364mg sodium, 76g carb, 2g fiber, 45g sugar, 9g protein

6 DESSERTS

GRILLED BLACKBERRY COBBLER

Serves 6

Indirect grilling is the key with this recipe. You must not grill this cobbler directly over the heat source. Place it off to the side, where you get indirect heat and cook the entire recipe evenly. No need to fire up the oven in your home to enjoy a great cobbler!

Instructions:

1. Preheat grill to 350°F (medium setting).

2. Place blackberries in a deep, round 10-inch aluminum foil pan. In a medium bowl, stir together sugar and flour. Add milk and melted butter and stir well. Pour mixture over berries.

3. Place foil pan over indirect heat and grill, with grill lid closed, for 1 hour. Remove from grill and enjoy with your favorite vanilla ice cream or vanilla frozen yogurt!

ABOVE:

It's hard to get Brooke to share her blackberry cobbler!

Grill

You'll Need

- ▸ 3 cups fresh blackberries
- ▸ 1 cup granulated sugar
- ▸ 1 cup self-rising flour
- ▸ 1 cup 2% milk
- ▸ 1/3 cup melted butter

MAKE IT LIGHTER

Blackberries are packed with numerous plant nutrients such as vitamins, minerals, and antioxidants.

332 calories
11g fat

(8g sat fat), 30mg chol, 363mg sodium, 57g carb, 2g fiber, 37g sugar, 4g protein

Before
433 calories
19g fat

(13g sat fat), 53mg chol, 413mg sodium, 64g carb, 2g fiber, 44g sugar, 2g protein

Goodness." Team Masterbuilt makes our company successful and I've always thought they deserve to share in our blessings. Each year at the Masterbuilt Christmas party I love to share a good meal, a fun evening, and cool gifts. Last year, I challenged them to meet a particular goal and promised if they met the goal we would have a huge reward. They met the goal and I kept my promise. When it came time for the Christmas party, we passed out Masterbuilt logo backpacks. I'm sure they were grateful for the backpacks, but I had something way more exciting in store. I announced that whoever had the number 8 on a piece of paper in the backpack won an all-expenses paid cruise to the Bahamas for them and a guest. The excitement grew as I counted

down from 3 to 2 to 1 and they all opened their backpacks. Every single employee had the number 8! It took them a minute or two to process the fact that the entire company was going on the cruise!

Once the shock wore off, it filled my heart with joy as each of them thanked my family immensely for the gift. Although Team Masterbuilt thinks they are blessed, what I hope they know is this—I'm the one who is blessed. Sharing the goodness with them means so much more to me than they will ever know.

So whether it's sharing with your own family and friends, sharing with your co-workers, or sharing with perfect strangers in need, I hope you're inspired to "Share the Goodness" in your own way.

OPPOSITE LEFT: Thanksgiving dinner with the Chapman Family
OPPOSITE RIGHT: Masterbuilt Christmas Party
ABOVE: Team Masterbuilt Grillin' for the Gulf
RIGHT: Donating a smoker to the Charlotte Rescue Mission

ROAD TRIP

For most folks, a road trip happens every once in a while—whether it be a family vacation, a tour of potential colleges, or a journey to move from one place to another. For me, life is one long road trip! In the early days at Masterbuilt, I would travel as a product salesman. As the company grew, I was able to bring on more salesmen and reps who took on territories and grew our business. Once our products and cookbooks were sold worldwide, there came a day when we decided to dip our toe into the media world. That dip became a full-on deep-sea dive into television, radio, and online media and it's been exciting! I'm so fortunate that my wife Tonya is able to travel with me and share in all of these experiences. It's even better on the occasions when my children can come along for the ride. From segments on regional news channels to cooking on live national television, we've made some awesome memories.

When you spend as much time on the road as we do, you have to get creative at mealtimes. When we toured to promote our first two cookbooks, we would eat food from our cooking segments and then rely on fast food drive-thrus and vending machines between destinations. As you can imagine, eating that way takes a toll on your waistline and your health! My family and my team have all tried to make healthier on-the-go eating choices. We've started carrying fruit and nuts for snacks and we split entrees at dinner. Portion control has been a huge part of it and we're all making adjustments. This go-round, I'm glad we're cooking lighter versions of all of our favorite recipes. I won't feel as guilty when I partake after a cooking segment, knowing it's a dadgum good AND healthy choice!

RECIPE NOTES & NUTRITION FACTS

Many of the recipes in this book were developed to be lighter and healthier than some of the original recipes. This means they may contain fewer calories, less fat, less salt, less sugar, or more fiber. At the bottom of each page, you will see that each recipe has been analyzed to determine the nutritional content of the recipe or recipes. To help you understand what the values mean in these nutritional analyses, we recommend that you compare them to the FDA's recommended values.

The following are the FDA's daily recommendations for an adult eating a 2000 calorie per day diet. You can refer to these numbers as you are looking at the nutritional values of the recipes in this book. Of course if you are a larger or active person, you probably have higher nutritional needs, and if you are a smaller or sedentary person, you probably have lower nutritional needs. In addition, children, and pregnant and lactating women have unique nutritional needs.

▶ FDA DAILY RECOMMENDATIONS FOR THE AVERAGE AMERICAN ADULT

Total Calories:	2000 calories
Total Fat:	65g
(Saturated Fat):	20g
Cholesterol:	300mg
Sodium:	2400mg
Carbohydrates:	300g
Fiber:	25g
Sugar:	No current recommendation, but lower is better
Protein:	50g

▶ NUTRITIONAL ANALYSIS ABBREVIATION KEY

calories
fat
sat fat = saturated fat
chol = cholesterol
sodium
carb = carbohydrates
fiber
sugar
protein

▶ CALCULATING THE NUTRITIONAL ANALYSIS WHEN USING THE FOLLOWING

▶ **For marinades:** We assume much is discarded when calculating the nutritional analysis.

▶ **For rubs:** Some recipes call for making more rub mixture than is used. The nutritional analysis is based on what was actually used.

▶ **For brines:** We assume that about 10% to 20% of the brine ingredients actually absorbs into the meat—depending on the type of meat and time in the brine.

▶ **For sauces:** When testing the recipes, we based the nutritional analysis on the amount of sauce that was actually used per serving, not including extra leftover sauce.

▶ A NOTE ABOUT APPLIANCES USED IN THIS BOOK

Although we include instructions for using our Masterbuilt products for these recipes, you can enjoy them with your own smokers, grills, fryers or steamers/boilers, no matter the brand name. Simply follow your own product instructions. Enjoy!

INDEX

ACKNOWLEDGEMENTS

This cookbook tells the story of the continued journey of my family sharing our stories and good food. The development teams from Oxmoor House and Time Home Inc. took recipes from my first two cookbooks, "DADGUM That's Good!"™ and "DADGUM That's Good, Too!"™ and helped me redevelop them in a healthier way for you to enjoy.

My wife Tonya worked tirelessly to compile our memories and photographs to help me share our stories with you.

I want to thank all my family, friends, and the team at Masterbuilt for sharing recipes and for always being willing taste-testers.

I also want to thank Alicia McGlamory for developing and testing recipes and writing the stories for me.

ABOVE:
Alicia and her husband Gary with me and Tonya at the Masterbuilt Christmas Party